YOU'RE OFFICER MATERIAL

A Veteran's SSB Interview Guide

Lessons and Secrets That Help SSB Aspirants Succeed with Clarity, Communication, and Character

By

Capt. Pradeepkumar K.P. (Retd.)
PRADEEPKUMAR K PADMANABHAN

DEDICATED TO

The young men and women who carry the dream of serving the nation in their hearts—
and to **the mentors** who help light the path.
This book is for you.

Table Of Contents

FOREWORD

It is a matter of great personal pride to write the foreword for You're Officer Material, a work authored by one of my most dependable and upright officers—Captain Pradeepkumar K.P. (Retd.). I had the privilege of commanding him during our service together in an Armoured Workshop in Punjab, and I can say with full conviction that he exemplified the very values this book now seeks to pass on to a new generation of aspirants.

Captain Pradeepkumar brought to the table more than just technical competence; he brought clarity of mind, strength of character, and an unwavering sense of purpose. His approach to service was sincere, structured, and selfless—qualities that remain at the core of what the Indian Armed Forces look for in an officer.

This book is a timely and essential guide—not only for those preparing to face the Service Selection Board (SSB), but for any individual aspiring to grow into a responsible, resilient, and respected citizen. It is grounded in lived experience, filled with personal anecdotes, and deeply insightful in how it navigates the reader through the mental, emotional, and moral preparation required to become a true leader.

What I find most admirable is that the book goes beyond procedural guidance. It doesn't just tell you how to crack the SSB; it invites you to discover who you are, and why you want to serve. It encourages aspirants to lead not through imitation, but through authenticity, awareness, and alignment with core values.

Captain Pradeepkumar has put together a thoughtful blend of military wisdom, practical advice, and personal reflection. His insights into clarity, character, and communication are not only relevant for future officers—they are relevant for all who aspire to lead with integrity, whether in uniform or not.

To all readers, I say this:

This book will not just prepare you for five days at a selection centre.It will prepare you for a lifetime of meaningful service, leadership, and duty.

I salute Captain Pradeepkumar for his continued contribution to nation-building, even beyond his uniformed service. May this book serve as a source of strength and direction for every aspirant who dares to dream and is ready to serve.

Brigadier Atul Mishra (Retd.)
Former Indian Army Officer

PREFACE

A Veteran's Note to the Aspirants

Dear Future Officer,

As I sit to pen down these words, memories from three decades ago flash before me—the excitement, the uncertainty, the silent prayers, and the unyielding spirit of a young man who dared to dream of wearing the uniform. That young man was me. And perhaps, today, it's you.

You're reading this book because something within you seeks not just a job, but a journey. A life of purpose, discipline, leadership, and service. Let me assure you—you are on a noble path, one that very few choose and even fewer complete. But if your heart is in it, and you're willing to do the work, this path will shape you into someone the nation can be proud of.

When I stood before the gates of the SSB for the first time, I had no guide, no strategy, and no real understanding of what was expected. I had only a dream and a deep desire to serve. I stumbled, I failed, and I learned the hard way. But every setback revealed a secret. Every failure whispered a lesson. And eventually, those whispers turned into the voice of success.

This book is a humble collection of those secrets—earned in sweat, molded in reflection, and shared with love. You will find techniques and tips, but more importantly, you will find truths. Not just about the SSB, but about yourself. Because the real preparation for the SSB isn't about learning tricks—it's about becoming the kind of person who naturally qualifies.

The Service Selection Board doesn't just assess your aptitude—it uncovers your attitude. It doesn't just test your knowledge—it reveals your nature. And in doing so, it selects not just officers, but leaders of character.

Whether you're on your first attempt or your last, know this—you're not alone. I've walked this road. And with this book, I walk it again, this time beside you.

Read it not just to pass an interview, but to discover the officer within. You're already Officer Material—you just have to believe it and bring it out.

With pride and faith in your journey,

- Capt. Pradeepkumar K.P. (Retd.)

Veteran | Engineer | Coach

INTRODUCTION

a) Why This Book Now?

The times have changed, but the core values that make an officer—courage, clarity, character, and commitment—remain timeless.

In recent years, I've seen a surge of passionate young men and women aspiring to join the Armed Forces. They come equipped with degrees, dreams, and digital information—but often, they lack direction. The internet is full of scattered tips, quick hacks, and recycled coaching advice, but very few resources speak from lived experience with depth, clarity, and honesty.

This book is my humble attempt to fill that gap.

As someone who walked the path with no Google, no YouTube mentors, and no shortcuts, I know what it feels like to chase the uniform with your heart full and your head confused. I also know what it takes to break through—not just the SSB process, but the inner limitations that hold us back.

So, why now?

Because today's aspirants need more than mock interviews and model answers. They need mindset, mentorship, and meaning. They need to understand not just *what to do*, but *why it matters*.

They need stories that inspire, insights that clarify, and strategies that work—not just in the interview room, but in life.

This book brings together the classic lessons that stood the test of time and the modern approach that connects with today's youth. It's designed to help you think like an officer, act like a leader, and grow like a warrior—from the inside out.

I wrote this because I believe India needs more officers—not just in uniform, but in spirit. And if you're holding this book, you're already on your way.

This is more than a guide. It's a conversation. A reflection. A transformation.

And it's exactly the book I wish I had when I began.

Let's begin your mission.

Your journey to becoming officer material starts now.

b) Officer Material: More Than Just a Phrase

What does it mean when someone says, *"You're officer material"*?

Is it just a compliment, or does it carry something deeper— something sacred?

Over the years, I've heard this phrase used in many ways:

At coaching academies, in SSB centers, during interviews, and even among friends trying to motivate one another. But very few pause to ask—what truly defines an officer, beyond the uniform, beyond the selection?

Being *Officer Material* is not about having the perfect resume or the smartest answers. It's not even about physical fitness or fluent English. It's about embodying a mindset—a way of thinking, responding, and living that reflects courage, clarity, and commitment to a cause bigger than oneself.

It's about:

- Leading without ego

- Acting with integrity even when no one is watching

- Taking responsibility when things go wrong, and giving credit when they go right

- Staying calm under pressure and composed in chaos

- Inspiring others not just with words, but by example

Officer Material is not born—it's built. It's a choice you make every single day: to grow, to rise, to serve, and to stand up for what's right, no matter the odds.

In this book, you'll read about the official tasks and tests that evaluate "officer-like qualities" (OLQs). But more importantly, you'll learn how to build those qualities within yourself, naturally and authentically.

Because here's the truth—if you live like an officer, speak like an officer, and think like an officer, selection is no longer an accident—it becomes inevitable.

So the next time someone says *"You're officer material,"* don't take it lightly.

It's not just praise. It's a reminder of the potential you carry—and the standard you're meant to uphold.

And if no one's said it yet, let me be the first:

Yes, you are Officer Material.

Now let's prove it—together.

c) A Journey from Aspirant to Officer

Every officer once stood where you are today—unsure, eager, hopeful, and perhaps a little nervous.

The journey from aspirant to officer is not just about clearing an interview or passing a fitness test. It's about transformation. It's about shedding the ordinary and stepping into a life of extraordinary purpose.

For me, it began in a small town, with nothing more than a dream and determination. No special background, no elite coaching, and no shortcuts. Just a fire inside—to wear the olive green, to serve with pride, and to become something more than I had ever imagined.

And like most aspirants, my journey wasn't straight.

I faced failures.

I faced rejections.

I faced doubt—both from within and from the world around me.

But with each setback, I chose to rise. I chose to reflect, refine, and return stronger. With every failed attempt, I was unknowingly carving the version of myself that *was meant to be an officer*—one who could face discomfort with dignity, pressure with presence, and decisions with decisiveness.

That is what the Armed Forces are looking for—not perfection, but potential. Not brilliance alone, but balance. Not just answers, but authenticity.

When I finally stood in front of the board that selected me, I wasn't acting or performing. I was simply being who I had become through that journey—a person ready to lead, ready to serve, and ready to carry the nation's trust on my shoulders.

This book is my offering to you—a fellow aspirant on this sacred path. It's not written to impress you. It's written to equip you—with tools, stories, strategies, and most importantly, the perspective that transforms pressure into purpose.

If you've made the choice to walk this path, I promise—this journey will shape you like no other.

And one day, when you look back from the other side, you will realize:

"I didn't just become an officer. I became the best version of myself."

And that, my friend, is a victory worth every effort.

Part I: The Call of the Uniform

Chapter 1

1. A NOBLE CAREER: WHY CHOOSE THE ARMED FORCES?

In a world full of career choices—some driven by money, some by convenience, and others by social status—there stands a path that calls for something deeper: courage, conviction, and character. That path leads to the Armed Forces.

Choosing to serve in the Indian Armed Forces is not just selecting a job; it's embracing a way of life. One where the stakes are real, the values are non-negotiable, and the rewards are far beyond a paycheck.

Yes, the pay, perks, and privileges are good—and they've only improved over the years. But ask any officer, and they'll tell you: it's not the money that keeps them going. It's the honour.

The honour of leading men into uncertainty with clarity.

The honour of standing tall when others sit in comfort.

The honour of being the first to respond in a crisis—and the last to retreat.

In Kohima, Nagaland, on a war memorial lies an inscription that reads:

"When you go home, tell them of us and say,

For your tomorrow, we gave our today."

These words aren't just etched in stone. They're etched in the hearts of every soldier who has ever stood guard while the rest of the country slept peacefully.

The words engraved prominently at the entrance of the Chetwode Hall, which is the main administrative and ceremonial building of the Indian Military Academy (IMA), Dehradun. The Chetwode Credo:

The safety, honour and welfare of your country come first, always and every time.

The honour, welfare and comfort of the men you command come next.

Your own ease, comfort and safety come last, always and every time."

It has become the spiritual and ethical backbone of officer training in India.

So, why choose the Armed Forces?

- Because you believe in something bigger than yourself.

- Because you want a life that demands your best every single day.

- Because you want to lead, serve, protect, and inspire.

- Because you want your life to matter—not just to you, but to your nation.

It is the only career that shapes you completely—physically, mentally, emotionally, and spiritually. It doesn't just give you a rank. It gives you an identity. A brotherhood. A legacy.

And even if you serve for a few years, the Armed Forces leave a mark on you that no other institution can. You walk out with discipline, leadership, resilience, and confidence that the corporate world highly values and actively seeks.

So if your heart beats a little faster at the sight of the uniform...

If your chest swells with pride when the national anthem plays...

If you want to be the difference, not just talk about it...

Then yes, my friend—you belong here.

This is not just a career. It is a calling.

And if you're listening closely,

the call may already be ringing.

1.1. Honour, Purpose, and Perks

When most people think about the Armed Forces, they often ask: *"What do you get?"*

But the better question is: *"Who do you become?"*

Because joining the Armed Forces gives you more than a career—it gives you honour, purpose, and yes, some of the finest perks any profession can offer.

Honour: The Unspoken Reward

Honour cannot be measured in currency or counted in benefits. It's the silent pride you carry when the uniform hugs your chest. It's the respect people offer you—not just because of what you do, but because of what you represent.

As an officer, you become a symbol of discipline, leadership, and courage. You are trusted with decisions that affect lives, communities, and at times, the nation. This trust is sacred—and it is earned through your integrity, actions, and example.

Purpose: Living for Something Larger Than Yourself

While many chase careers that serve their own ambitions, an officer lives for a cause greater than self. You're not just clocking hours—you're safeguarding peace, leading in crisis, and being the calm in chaos.

Your days are fueled by meaning, not monotony. Your role isn't just a job—it's a mission. Whether you're on the field, at the border, in disaster relief, or training the next generation—you know your work matters.

And that kind of purpose... it changes how you walk, talk, and think for the rest of your life.

Perks: More Than Meets the Eye

Yes, the Armed Forces come with unmatched benefits:

- Excellent pay scales and regular promotions

- Generous allowances (field, travel, uniform, high-altitude, etc.)

- Fully covered medical care for you and your family

- Subsidized housing and canteen facilities

- Lifetime pension and post-retirement support

- Opportunities for global training, advanced studies, and UN missions

But perhaps the biggest perk is the quality of life—the camaraderie, the security, the structured growth, and the respect that follows you long after retirement.

So yes, the Armed Forces do offer perks. But more importantly, they offer a life of dignity.

A life where every morning feels purposeful, and every night is slept with satisfaction.

"The uniform may be stitched in cloth,

But it's worn in the soul."

If that's the life you seek,

You're not just applying for a career—you're answering a calling.

1.2. True Stories of Service and Sacrifice

Behind every medal pinned to a uniform lies a story—not just of courage, but of character. And behind every flag-draped coffin lies a legacy—not of death, but of undying devotion.

The Armed Forces don't just train you for war. They teach you what it means to give, lead, and serve without hesitation. And in doing so, they produce stories that inspire generations—not just within the defence community, but across the nation.

Here are a few glimpses into such stories—real, raw, and unforgettable:

When Duty Becomes Legacy, and Service Becomes Immortal

The strength of a nation does not lie in its weapons alone.

It lies in the unseen courage, relentless service, and quiet sacrifice of its people—especially those in uniform.

This chapter brings you true stories—not just of battlefield bravery, but of those who have shown extraordinary character, compassion, and service throughout their careers. Some of them received medals. Most never sought recognition. But all of them lived the spirit of "Service Before Self."

Captain Vikram Batra, PVC (Posthumous)

Captain Vikram Batra, PVC (Posthumous), of 13 JAK Rifles, became the face of unmatched bravery during the Kargil War of 1999. At just 24 years old, he led his men through treacherous terrain and intense enemy fire to capture Point 5140 in one of the war's most iconic operations. His now-famous radio call, "Yeh Dil Maange More!", symbolized not just victory, but the fire in his soul to keep going. Days later, while rescuing a wounded comrade during the assault on Point 4875, he was fatally hit. His final act was not of glory, but of love—for his brother-in-arms and for the tricolour he wore on his chest.

Captain Batra's story teaches us that leadership is not about shouting commands—it's about living your values in the line of fire. He led from the front, inspired with heart, and never hesitated to put his life on the line for his men. For every SSB aspirant and future officer, his life is a shining example of what it means to be truly officer material—fearless, selfless, and forever faithful to the call of duty.

Subedar Major (Honorary Captain) Yogendra Singh Yadav, PVC

He was just 19 years old when he etched his name in history as one of the youngest recipients of the Param Vir Chakra—India's highest wartime gallantry award. During the Kargil War, he was part of the Ghatak Platoon tasked with capturing Tiger Hill, a near-impossible mission under heavy Pakistani fire. Despite being hit by multiple bullets while scaling a vertical cliff face, he continued to climb, lobbed grenades into enemy bunkers, and cleared the path for his team to capture the peak. Though severely wounded and presumed dead, he survived—his grit outlasting even the battle itself.

Yogendra Singh Yadav's story is not just one of physical courage, but of mental clarity, unwavering resolve, and absolute devotion to duty. He embodies the spirit of a true soldier—one who doesn't stop when he's hurt, but only when the mission is complete. For SSB aspirants and future officers, his journey is a reminder that real officer-like qualities are forged in moments of silence, pain, and personal sacrifice—when no one is watching, and yet everything depends on your choice to keep moving forward.

CQMH Abdul Hamid, PVC (Posthumous)

In the 1965 Indo-Pak war, amidst the blistering tank battlefields of Asal Uttar (Punjab), one man stood between the enemy and victory—CQMH Abdul Hamid, a humble quartermaster of the Grenadiers Regiment. Armed with only a recoilless gun mounted on a jeep, Hamid single-handedly destroyed seven enemy Patton tanks, displaying incredible courage, precision, and composure under fire. His bravery changed the tide of the battle and earned him the Param Vir Chakra, India's highest wartime gallantry award.

Abdul Hamid's actions weren't born out of training alone—they came from an unshakable sense of duty, patriotism, and fearless leadership, even without the badge of an officer. He made the ultimate sacrifice on the battlefield, but left behind a legacy that teaches aspirants that rank is not required to show leadership—character is. His story is a living reminder that true warriors rise from simplicity, serve with humility, and leave behind immortal courage.

Lt Gen Zorawar Chand Bakshi, MVC, VrC, PVSM,VSM

He was the most decorated General in the history of the Indian Army—a soldier who served with distinction in almost every major conflict India faced from World War II to the liberation of Bangladesh. Known for his daring leadership in the 1947–48 Kashmir operations, his brilliance in the 1965 Indo-Pak War, and his strategic role in the 1971 Bangladesh War, Gen Bakshi embodied courage, decisiveness, and aggressive battlefield command. His planning and execution in capturing the Haji Pir Pass earned him the Maha Vir Chakra, and his troops revered him for never asking them to do what he wouldn't do himself.

What made Lt Gen Bakshi extraordinary wasn't just the battles he won, but the ethos he carried—relentless preparation, fearless initiative, and total commitment to the mission and his men. He believed that a true leader leads from the front, in mud, in fire, and in silence. For SSB aspirants and future officers, his life is a blueprint for what it means to be not just a commander, but a soldier first—always visible, always responsible, and always ready.

Lt Gen Sagat Singh, PVSM

One of the most decisive and daring generals in Indian military history, Lt Gen Sagat Singh, PVSM, led from the front not with noise, but with sheer strategic brilliance. As the Commander of IV Corps during the 1971 Indo-Pak war, he executed one of the boldest moves in modern warfare—airlifting troops across the heavily defended Meghna River using helicopters. This unprecedented heliborne operation allowed Indian forces to bypass strongholds, maintain momentum, and liberate Dhaka in just thirteen days. His vision, speed, and decisiveness played a critical role in Pakistan's surrender and the birth of Bangladesh.

Known as a soldier's general, Lt Gen Sagat Singh was admired by peers like Gen Sam Manekshaw for his clarity of command and quiet courage. He believed in initiative, empowered his juniors, and redefined leadership not by following orders blindly, but by creating opportunities when they didn't exist. His story is a timeless lesson for every aspirant—that true officer-like qualities lie in bold thinking, calm execution, and selfless service, even under the most unpredictable circumstances.

Major General (Dr.) A. P. Singhal, SM, VSM (AMC)

He was a distinguished officer in the Indian Army Medical Corps, known not only for his excellence in military medicine but also for his visionary leadership in health services within the Armed Forces. Decorated with the Sena Medal and Vishisht Seva Medal for his meritorious service, Gen. Singhal served in both operational and peacetime roles with distinction. His dedication to the physical and psychological well-being of soldiers, especially in high-stress and high-altitude environments, earned him deep respect across ranks.

Beyond his decorated military career, Major General Singhal was also a renowned medical educator, administrator, and public health thinker, continuing to serve India's health systems post-retirement. He believed in a holistic approach to soldier welfare—one that nurtured body, mind, and spirit. His legacy is a powerful reminder that the Armed Forces are not just defended by rifles, but also by doctors in uniform who heal, lead, and protect with equal courage. For every defence aspirant, his life offers a model of service beyond the stethoscope—and leadership beyond the rank.

Col. V.R. Mohan (Retd.): The Farmer Soldier

He exemplifies the ideal that service to the nation doesn't end with retirement—it evolves into deeper community impact. After an illustrious career in the Indian Army, Col. Mohan returned to his native village and turned his focus to rural development and youth empowerment. Transforming barren land into a thriving organic farm, he not only revived local agriculture but also created employment and training opportunities for ex-servicemen and village youth. His leadership in the civil sector became an extension of his military values—discipline, vision, and selfless action.

Col. Mohan's post-retirement mission reflects what it truly means to be an officer for life. Instead of resting on his past, he chose to apply his leadership for the betterment of society, embodying the idea that real officers don't just lead on the battlefield—they uplift wherever they stand. For every SSB aspirant, his life is a reminder that the uniform may be worn for a few decades, but the responsibility it instills lasts forever.

Naik Rambeer Singh Tomar, AC (Posthumous)

He was a brave non-commissioned officer from the 15 Kumaon Regiment, serving on deputation with 26 Rashtriya Rifles in Jammu & Kashmir. On 3 March 2001, during a high-risk search-and-destroy operation in Doda district, he volunteered to lead his team into a house occupied by terrorists. Displaying extraordinary courage and skill, he eliminated four terrorists single-handedly—two with grenades and two in close-quarters combat—even after sustaining a serious wound near his eye. Though gravely injured, he continued fighting until the threat was neutralized, ensuring the safety of his comrades.

For his conspicuous bravery, leadership under fire, and complete self-sacrifice, Naik Rambeer Singh Tomar was posthumously awarded the Ashok Chakra, India's highest peacetime gallantry honour. His actions exemplify the highest qualities of an officer-like mindset—initiative, unwavering courage, and loyalty to the mission—even without formal rank. His legacy is a powerful lesson for every aspirant: that true officer material reveals itself not through position, but through action and resolve.

Major Sandeep Unnikrishnan, AC (Posthumous)

He was a National Security Guard (NSG) commando who laid down his life during the 2008 Mumbai terrorist attacks, displaying exceptional courage and unmatched leadership. A graduate of the NDA and IMA, he was known for his calm demeanor and sharp tactical mind. During Operation Black Tornado, he led his team into the besieged Taj Mahal Palace Hotel to rescue hostages. Even after one of his team members was injured, he pressed forward, engaging the terrorists directly. He was martyred in the line of duty, but not before saving several lives and striking fear into the hearts of the attackers.

His last recorded words—"Don't come up, I'll handle them"—echo through the halls of heroism in India's military history. Major Sandeep's life reminds every aspirant that true bravery is silent, focused, and selfless. He didn't seek glory; he chose to act. His sacrifice is a timeless example of what it means to be an officer—not just trained to fight, but committed to protect, lead, and if needed, lay down one's life without hesitation. For every future officer, he remains a symbol of courage, clarity, and the ultimate call of duty.

Flying Officer Nirmal Jit Singh Sekhon, PVC (Posthumous)

He remains a legend in the Indian Air Force—a young pilot whose valor during the 1971 Indo-Pak War redefined aerial courage. Stationed at Srinagar airbase, he took off in his Gnat fighter jet amidst a surprise attack by six Pakistani Sabre jets. Undeterred by being outnumbered, he engaged the enemy head-on in a dogfight that showcased exceptional skill, presence of mind, and raw bravery. He succeeded in shooting down two enemy aircraft before being shot down himself. He made the ultimate sacrifice, but not before saving countless lives on the ground.

Flying Officer Sekhon's heroism is etched not just in war history but in the spirit of the Indian Air Force. He exemplified the highest traditions of duty, self-sacrifice, and unshakable commitment, even when the odds were impossibly stacked. For every young defence aspirant, his story is a shining beacon of what it means to rise above fear, put mission before life, and live on forever through one's actions. His life reminds us that true officer-like qualities often shine brightest in the face of impossible choices.

Lieutenant Triveni Singh, AC (Posthumous)

An officer of the Rajputana Rifles who laid down his life in 2004, displaying extraordinary courage during a fidayeen (suicide) attack on Jammu Railway Station. Off duty and posted as the Adjutant of his unit, he volunteered to lead a quick reaction team when the terror attack was reported. On reaching the scene, he assessed the situation quickly and engaged the terrorists in close combat, neutralizing both attackers and saving the lives of over 300 civilians trapped inside the station. Even after being grievously injured, he continued fighting until the last threat was eliminated.

Lt. Triveni Singh's heroism reflects the truest spirit of an officer—decisive in action, fearless in sacrifice, and unwavering in duty. He was known for his quiet discipline and sharp intellect, but in his final moments, it was his will to protect others at all cost that defined him. For every SSB aspirant, his life is a call to remember that leadership is not about stars on your shoulders, but the strength in your choices—especially when time is short and danger is near.

The list of such heroes is long, and their stories are endless.

Unsung Heroes: Everyday Acts of Service

For every headline hero, there are thousands of unnamed soldiers—guarding borders in minus 40°C, conducting rescue missions during floods, building bridges in disaster zones, and standing as the last line of defence when everything else fails.

Their faces may never be known. But their spirit lives on in every Indian flag that flies high.

NCOs and Junior Leaders: The Backbone of the Forces

Let's not forget the countless JCOs, NCOs, and jawans who silently carry the load of operations, logistics, training, and morale—often unnoticed.

Nursing Staff & Support Units — who serve during floods, earthquakes, and pandemics, not for glory but out of sheer duty.

What These Stories Teach Us
That bravery is not just about gunfire—it's about standing firm in chaos.

That service doesn't end with retirement—it evolves into new forms.

That sacrifice isn't always visible—but always valuable.

"You don't need a medal to make a difference. You just need a mindset."

As you prepare for the SSB:

Let these stories humble and strengthen you.

Let them remind you why you chose this path.

Let them guide your preparation—not with pressure, but with purpose.

Because in the end, you're not just preparing for a test.

You're preparing to be worthy of those who served before you, and to carry the legacy forward—with clarity, character, and commitment.

What These Stories Teach Us

- Service is not about glory—it's about grit.

- Sacrifice is not about dying—it's about living with purpose, whatever the cost.

- Courage is not about being fearless—it's about rising despite fear.

You don't need to wear the uniform yet to be inspired by their example.

But if you truly want to honour them, carry their values forward.

Live with clarity.

Lead with conviction.

And serve, not because you must—but because you choose to.

Because one day, your story may be the one that inspires the next generation

1.3. Officers – Army, Air Force, Navy: Understanding the Pathways

When you first decide to join the Armed Forces, one of the biggest questions is:

"How do I enter?"

The good news? India offers multiple entry routes to become a commissioned officer—each tailored to different stages of your academic and personal journey.

Let's break them down:

1. National Defence Academy (NDA) – Army, Navy & Air Force

For: 10+2 (PCM for Air Force/Navy)

Exam: NDA Exam by UPSC + SSB + Medical

Age: 16½ to 19½ years

Training: NDA Khadakwasla (3 yrs) + IMA (Army), AFA (Air Force), INA (Navy)

Commission: Permanent Commission (Lieutenant / Flying Officer / Sub Lieutenant)

2. Technical Entry Scheme (TES) – Army Only

For: 10+2 with PCM (minimum 60%) + JEE Mains

No written exam; shortlisted for SSB directly

Age: 16½ to 19½ years

Training: OTA Gaya + Military Engineering Colleges

Commission: Permanent Commission in Technical Branches

3. Combined Defence Services (CDS) – All Three Forces

For: Graduates (any stream for Army; BSc/Engineering for Navy/Air Force)

Exam: CDS by UPSC + SSB + Medical

Age: 19–24 (Army), 19–22 (Navy), 19–24 (Air Force)

Academies:

IMA Dehradun (Army – PC)

INA Ezhimala (Navy – PC)

AFA Hyderabad (Air Force – PC)

OTA Chennai (Army – SSC, Male & Female)

Commission: Permanent or Short Service, depending on academy

4. AFCAT (Air Force Common Admission Test) – Air Force Only

For: Graduates (Flying Branch), Engineers (Ground Duty)

Conducted by: Indian Air Force (twice a year)

Age:

Flying: 19–24

Ground Duty: 20–26

Branches: Flying, Ground Duty (Technical/Non-Tech), Meteorology

Commission: Short Service (Flying), PC/SSC in other branches

5. INET (Indian Navy Entrance Test) – Navy Only

For: Graduates & Engineers

Exam: INET + SSB (May be merged with CDS entries now)

Commission: SSC and PC entries in Executive, Engineering, Education branches

6. NCC Special Entry (Army, Navy, Air Force)

For: NCC C Certificate holders (Army Senior Division/Naval/Air Wing)

No written exam, direct SSB interview

Commission: Mostly Short Service (few PC)

7. JAG Entry (Army Legal Branch)

For: Law Graduates (LLB, enrolled with Bar Council)

Direct SSB

Age: 21–27

Commission: Short Service Commission

8. University Entry Scheme (UES) / SSC Tech / TGC

For: Engineering students/graduates

Direct SSB (No written exam)

Applies to: All 3 Forces (based on scheme)

Commission: Technical arms and branches

9. Women Entries

Women can join the Armed Forces via:

NDA (from 2021 onwards)

CDS (OTA Chennai – SSC)

AFCAT

NCC Special Entry

JAG, SSC Tech, Education branches

10. Internal Commissioning & Departmental Entries

Serving personnel (jawans/airmen/sailors) can appear for:

ACC (Army Cadet College)

PC (SL), SCO, and other in-service commissioning programs

No matter the entry route—the selection is rigorous, the training is tough, and the honour is unmatched. Choose your path based on your age, qualification, and calling. And remember, what matters more than when you enter... is how you grow once you're in.

"Different roads, one destination—to serve, to lead, to become an officer of the Indian Armed Forces."

Chapter 2

2. MY SSB JOURNEY: FROM REJECTIONS TO RECOMMENDATIONS

Every officer has a story. Mine began not with success—but with setbacks.

The dream to wear the uniform and serve the nation started early for me. As a young boy, I was mesmerized by the crisp uniforms, the poise of men in uniform, and the stories of honour and adventure shared by my uncle, who worked closely with the Armed Forces. The Armed Forces weren't just a career in my eyes—they were a calling.

I first attempted the NDA written exam straight after my intermediate exams. I gave it everything I had—but I failed. Around the same time, I received two opportunities: one to join the Indian Air Force as an airman, and another to begin my engineering degree. I chose to complete my engineering, with a clear mission—to come back stronger and attempt a direct entry into the Forces as a commissioned officer.

But it wasn't smooth.

I will take you through the trials, tribulations, and transformation I experienced across two unsuccessful SSB attempts and how, in the third, I walked out with the recommendation that would change my life. These aren't just stories of interviews and test results—these are stories of internal battles, lessons in self-awareness, and the slow, deliberate shaping of the officer within me. I will share the mistakes I made, the feedback I received, the changes I embraced, and the shift in mindset that made all the difference.

2.1. First Steps: NDA Dreams

Every great journey begins with a spark. For me, it was the sight of crisp uniforms, the commanding presence of officers, and the stories of discipline and adventure shared by my uncle—a Master Technician at Hindustan Aeronautics Limited (HAL). His deep connection with the Armed Forces stirred something in me. It wasn't just admiration. It was aspiration.

Even as a schoolboy, I was fascinated by the life of the soldier—structured, purposeful, and full of courage. I wanted to learn languages, meet people from across the country, and live a life beyond the ordinary. I dreamed of joining the Indian Army, and the first real gateway I saw was through three letters etched into every defence aspirant's mind: NDA.

The Dream Takes Shape

As soon as I completed my intermediate exams, I applied for the NDA (National Defence Academy) exam. I still remember holding that admit card like it was a ticket to destiny. I studied hard, prayed harder, and stepped into the exam hall with more hope than confidence.

But I didn't make it.

The result hit me like a wave. For a teenager who pinned everything on that one chance, the failure felt heavy. But somewhere inside, the dream didn't die. It just took a new shape. And fate, as it often does, opened multiple doors simultaneously.

Two Letters, One Decision

Around the same time, I received two life-changing call letters:

1. One from the Indian Air Force—to join as an airman in the technical stream.

2. The other, from an engineering college in Kerala—offering me admission to pursue a B.Tech degree.

It was a tough choice. On one hand, a guaranteed start in the Forces. On the other, a longer path that could potentially lead me to become a commissioned officer. I chose the latter. Not because it was easier—but because it aligned with my deeper goal:

"If I'm going to wear the uniform, I want to earn the stars on my shoulder."

And so, I stepped into the world of engineering—with the military still on my mind, and the badge of an officer still in my heart.

The Dream Evolves, Not Ends

My NDA dream may not have come true in the way I imagined. But it planted the seed.

A seed that would grow through rejections, reflections, mentors, and ultimately, a recommendation that changed my life.

That's what I want you to understand:

Not clearing NDA is not the end. It's just the beginning of a different path—with the same destination.

If you couldn't make it to NDA, don't lose heart.

You haven't lost the dream—you've just changed the route. And trust me, every route has its lessons, blessings, and breakthroughs.

What matters is not how early you start, but how deeply you commit.

Because eventually, it's not just about entering the academy—it's about becoming the officer the academy would be proud to train

2.2. Lessons from Mysore & Allahabad

They say failure is a better teacher than success. Looking back, my first two SSB attempts—Mysore and Allahabad—taught me lessons that no coaching center ever could.

Each rejection hurt. But each one revealed something I needed to see, something I needed to grow into. These weren't just failed attempts—they were formative experiences that shaped me into the person who finally earned that recommendation letter.

Mysore SSB: Raw Passion Meets Harsh Reality

My first SSB call came for Mysore. I still remember the excitement in my heart as I packed my bag, neatly folded my call letter, and took the train with dreams of becoming an officer. I had no idea what to expect. No formal training. No real strategy.

But I was eager. And that counted for something.

I cleared the screening test, which gave me a surge of confidence. Out of around 200 aspirants, only about 30 moved to the next round—and I was grateful to be one of them.

But what followed humbled me.

The GTO tasks exposed my lack of preparation.

I fumbled during group planning.

I bruised my palms during a monkey jump obstacle.

And during the interview, when asked about the books I read, I nervously mentioned *Mein Kampf*—a book I happened to be reading at the time, without considering the impression it might leave.

The result? Not recommended.

Only one candidate made it—ironically, my own classmate.

But instead of being disheartened, I asked him for feedback. I wanted to know what worked for him, and what didn't work for me.

I walked away with my head held high—not because I succeeded, but because I started to understand the process. I saw my gaps clearly. I saw the areas I needed to work on. Most importantly, I realized:

You don't just show up at SSB—you grow into it.

Allahabad SSB: Awareness Without Expression

Three months later, I received another call—this time for SSB Allahabad. With the Mysore experience behind me, I felt better prepared.

And in many ways, I was.

I was familiar with the format, I knew what to carry, and I was mentally more composed. But something was still missing: fluency. Confidence. Communication.

During the group discussion and planning exercises, I found it hard to speak up. My thoughts were clear, but my words were stuck.

I hesitated. I overthought. I underperformed.

In the interview, I tried to play it safe. I gave well-mannered, cautious answers. But that very "safety" took away the authenticity of my personality. The interviewer even tested my nervousness by speaking in a low tone. I struggled to respond with confidence.

And just like that, I was back on the train home—again, without selection.

The twist? Not a single candidate from that batch was selected. A washed-out group.

But even in defeat, I found growth.

What These Attempts Taught Me

1. You can't fake OLQs – Officer-Like Qualities are not lines to memorize. They are values to live.

2. Confidence isn't noise—it's clarity – You don't need to shout. You just need to speak with conviction.

3. Communication is not just language—it's expression – You must connect thoughts to words, and words to energy.

4. Physical obstacles are nothing compared to mental ones – Fear, doubt, hesitation—those are the real barriers.

5. Feedback is a gift – After each failure, I reflected. I even asked selected candidates for advice. That helped more than any textbook.

Failure is Just a Filter

SSB doesn't reject you. It refines you. It puts a mirror in front of you and asks,

"Are you ready to lead? Or are you here to perform?"

It took two failures for me to start looking inward instead of outward. To stop trying to "clear" SSB and start becoming the person who naturally qualifies.

Mysore and Allahabad didn't close doors for me.

They opened a much bigger one—the one within.

And in that space, the real preparation began

I realized I needed a mentor, someone who could show me the mirror.

Meeting Lt. Col Bala: My Turning Point

In Bangalore, I met Lt. Col Bala, a seasoned officer and mentor. He didn't sugarcoat anything. He told me straight:

"You have potential, but you lack exposure. Your world is too small. Expand it."

He helped me identify my blind spots—poor communication, nervousness, lack of real-world awareness. But more importantly, he helped me rediscover my true personality.

He taught me how to reflect, speak with clarity, and express without fear. His guidance planted the seed of inner transformation and more understanding about SSB Testing.

2.3. Final Victory in Bhopal

By the time I received my SSB call letter for Bhopal, I wasn't the same man who had stumbled through Mysore and hesitated in Allahabad.

This time, I was calm, clear, and committed.

I had reflected on my past failures. I had worked on my communication, my awareness, and most importantly—my mindset. Thanks to the honest guidance of Lt. Col Bala, I finally understood:

"SSB isn't about impressing others—it's about expressing your authentic self with clarity and courage."

Arrival: Mind, Body & Soul in Sync

I arrived at Bhopal with a heart full of purpose and a mind free of anxiety. At the railway station, I joined the group of candidates waiting to be picked up. We were taken to the SSB premises in military vehicles—a small experience, but it already felt like I belonged.

After settling into the lines, we were called for screening the next morning. This time, I handled the Picture Perception and Discussion Test (PPDT) with poise. I didn't just narrate a story—I connected it to a real theme, and contributed meaningfully during the discussion.

I cleared the screening with ease.

Psychology Tests: Writing with Authenticity

In the psych tests—WAT, TAT, and SRT—I focused on being natural, not rehearsed. My sentences were positive, purposeful, and practical. I didn't write fairy tales or try to sound like a superhero. I simply responded as myself—someone who believes in doing the right thing with courage and care.

Even when faced with the blank slide in the TAT, I wrote a story rooted in social concern—because that's what I truly valued.

GTO Tasks: Leadership in Action

The GTO tasks were where I truly came alive. I gave creative inputs, supported my group members, and followed the rules without fail. In the individual obstacle round, I completed all 10 and repeated 4 more within the time limit—not out of desperation, but out of dedication.

In the Group Planning Exercise, I didn't try to dominate. I listened, suggested, and helped the group arrive at a workable solution. In the Lecturette, I spoke on a topic I truly resonated with, using a structure I had practiced: introduction, key points, conclusion.

There was no fear. Just flow.

Interview: Just Me, No Pretending

When my interview came, I treated it like a conversation. I answered honestly, stayed composed, and even when questions got tricky, I didn't panic. I acknowledged what I didn't know, shared what I believed in, and stayed consistent with everything I had written in my forms.

It wasn't perfect. But it was real. And that's what counts at the SSB.

The Moment of Truth

On the final day, we were all seated again in the hall where it had begun. The President of the Board addressed us, reminding us that not being selected wasn't the end—and that sometimes, life has other plans.

Then he announced:

"Only two have been selected."

The hall fell silent.

First name: *Chest No. 7 – Sushil Kumar Saini.*

Then... *Chest No. 12 – Pradeep Kumar K.P.*

My name.

I didn't jump. I didn't scream. I just smiled. Silently. Deeply.

Because I knew...

This wasn't just a result. This was a reward for every fall I had risen from.

This wasn't the end of a journey. It was the beginning of a life I had dreamed of.

I stayed back for the medicals. Submitted my certificates. Cleared all the formalities.

And within two months, I held a letter in my hand—an official call to join OTA Chennai for training.

That was the final proof that growth is never wasted. That your past doesn't define your future—your perseverance does.

To You, the Aspirant

If you've failed once... or even twice... don't stop.

Keep showing up. Keep improving. Keep believing.

Because one day, your name will be called.

And when it is, you'll realize:

"You were never being rejected. You were just being prepared."

Chapter 3

3. Learning from Defeat: Real Failures, Real Growth

Defeat doesn't feel good. Let's be honest.

It can bruise your ego, shake your confidence, and sometimes even make you question your dreams.

But here's the truth I learned the hard way:

Defeat is not the opposite of success. It is a part of success.

My SSB journey didn't begin with recommendations and applause—it began with silence, rejection slips, and unanswered prayers. I remember walking out of the Mysore and Allahabad SSB centers with a heavy heart, wondering what went wrong. I had given my best, hadn't I?

But as I matured through the process, I realized something important:

"Giving your best" is not just about effort—it's about direction, awareness, and reflection.

The Gift Hidden in Rejection

When you're rejected, especially in a process like the SSB, it's not a judgment on your worth as a human being. It's a signal. A redirection. A call to go deeper.

For me, every failed attempt gave birth to a better version of myself:

- I became more observant.

- I started listening to my tone, my body language, my attitude.

- I began to understand that the SSB was not looking for a rehearsed performer—it was looking for a genuine personality.

Defeat, then, became my teacher. And reflection became my most powerful tool.

Ego vs. Evolution

One of the biggest blocks to growth is ego. After my first rejection, I was tempted to blame the system, the assessors, or even my luck. But deep inside, I knew—something within me needed to change.

That shift in mindset was the turning point.

I stopped trying to prove I was "officer material."

I started becoming officer material—in how I thought, spoke, behaved, and led myself daily.

Growth Is Invisible… Until It Isn't

The frustrating part about personal growth is that it's often invisible.

You read more.

You speak better.

You feel calmer.

But there's no scoreboard… until the moment comes when someone else sees it too.

For me, that moment was in Bhopal. But before that, there were months of silent preparation, small victories, and internal shifts that nobody clapped for.

So if you've faced rejection—or if you're afraid of it—remember this:

"Success is not what you get when everything goes right.

Success is what you become after everything goes wrong."

What I Gained from Defeat (That Success Could Never Teach Me):

- Humility – I learned to listen, accept feedback, and stay grounded.

- Resilience – I showed up again, and again, and again.

- Clarity – I stopped guessing what the SSB wanted and started living my truth.

- Strength – Not just physical, but emotional and mental.

- Faith – In the process, and in myself.

From Your Defeats, Build Your Foundation

If you've failed before—good. That means you're trying.

Now, don't just try harder. Try smarter. Reflect, refine, and rise.

Let your defeats fuel your discipline. Let your pain shape your purpose.

Because when you finally wear that uniform, every setback will feel like a brick that built your foundation.

And when someone asks you, *"How did you make it?"*, you'll smile and say:

"I didn't just learn from my victories.

I was made by my failures."

3.1. Washed-Out Batches and Emotional Recovery

There's a unique kind of silence that fills the hall when the results are announced—and no one's name is called.

No applause.

No celebration.

Just a quiet realization: the entire batch has been washed out.

I experienced that at the Allahabad SSB. And let me tell you—it wasn't just disappointing. It was emotionally draining.

You invest your time, your effort, your energy—sometimes your entire identity—into those five days. And when the result is "no one selected," it's easy to feel like all of it was for nothing.

But it wasn't.

The Washout Doesn't Mean You're Not Worthy

SSB selection isn't a lottery. It's a carefully calibrated process designed to identify the right fit at the right time. When an entire batch is washed out, it doesn't mean you're all failures. It simply means that the board did not find the required alignment of qualities in that group at that moment.

It's tough to hear, I know. But that doesn't make it any less true.

In my case, I could've let the washout sink me into self-doubt.

Instead, I chose to do something rare: I reflected deeply.

- Why didn't I express myself fully in group tasks?

- Why did I feel frozen in the interview, trying to "get it right" instead of being real?

- Why did I struggle to connect my thoughts and words under pressure?

The answers were hard to admit—but they led to something powerful: clarity.

Emotional Recovery: The Inner Battle

We often talk about preparation for the SSB in terms of aptitude and fitness.

But no one talks enough about emotional recovery.

You see, every rejection leaves a residue. If you don't clean it, it clogs your spirit.

After the Allahabad experience, I allowed myself to feel the pain— but not stay in it. I journaled. I reflected. I had open conversations with those I trusted. I didn't suppress the disappointment, but I didn't let it define me either.

Because here's the truth:

"You're allowed to be upset after a rejection. You're not allowed to quit."

Use the Pain as Fuel

The emotional weight of rejection can either break you or build you. The choice is yours.

I used it to rebuild my mindset, refocus my energy, and recommit to the dream.

And when the next opportunity came—Bhopal—I stepped in with renewed purpose, not lingering pain.

What to Do If You Face a Washout:

1. Don't take it personally. It's about readiness, not rejection.

2. Talk about it. Share your experience with a mentor or peer. Don't isolate yourself.

3. Reflect on the process. Not just what you did—but *how* you felt during each task.

4. Write it down. Put your thoughts, reactions, and insights into a journal.

5. Take a break—then bounce back. Reset your emotional state before diving into prep again.

One Batch. One Result. Infinite Lessons.

The washed-out batch at Allahabad taught me that true growth happens in the shadows. When no one's watching, and when things don't go your way, that's when your character is tested.

And it's those silent, unseen moments of growth that eventually bring the loudest victories.

So, if you've been in a washed-out batch—or feel like life's washed you out—remember:

You're not out of the race.

You're just being seasoned for a better performance.

3.2. Meeting a Mentor: Lt. Col Bala's Impact

After two failed attempts at SSB—one marked by confusion, the other by silence—I stood at a crossroads.

I had the passion. I had the potential.

But I lacked something essential: perspective.

That's when life introduced me to Lt. Col Bala—a seasoned officer with the kind of presence that commanded respect without uttering a single word. We didn't meet in a formal coaching center. We met through life's design, at the right moment, when I needed him most.

And that meeting changed everything.

A Man Who Saw Through Me

From the very first conversation, Lt. Col Bala made one thing clear:

"You don't need to become someone else to clear SSB.

You need to discover who you truly are—and express that with confidence."

He wasn't interested in teaching me formulas or model answers. He was interested in helping me uncover the officer within.

In his presence, I didn't feel judged—I felt seen.

The Mirror I Needed

Lt. Col Bala was brutally honest, but never cruel. He told me, without sugarcoating:

- "You have limited exposure to the outside world."

- "Your communication lacks fluency—not because of language, but because of clarity."

- "You're trying too hard to impress. Stop performing. Start being real."

At first, his words stung. But I knew he was right.

No one had ever told me these things so directly—and so kindly.

He didn't just point out my weaknesses. He showed me how to work on them.

He helped me:

- Break down the psychological tests into thought processes, not just writing exercises.

- Understand the purpose behind every GTO task—not just what to do, but *why* it's done.

- Practice interview responses that came from truth, not templates.

- Rebuild my confidence—not by hype, but by clarity and consistency.

From Confused to Composed

With his mentorship, I didn't just improve—I transformed.

- I stopped fearing interviews. I started looking forward to them.

- I began to speak clearly, think deeply, and lead confidently in group settings.

- I no longer saw SSB as an exam. I saw it as a platform to be myself, fully and fearlessly.

And it worked.

In my very next attempt at Bhopal SSB, I didn't just survive—I thrived.

And when the results were declared, and my name was called, I silently thanked the man who helped me cross that invisible line between "trying" and becoming.

The Power of a True Mentor

Mentors don't give you answers.

They give you awareness.

They don't make the journey easier.

They help you make it worth it.

Lt. Col Bala didn't just help me clear the SSB.

He helped me become the kind of man who deserved to wear the uniform.

To Every Aspirant Reading This: Find Your Bala

You don't have to walk this path alone. Find someone who:

- Challenges your blind spots

- Believes in your potential

- Guides you with truth, not just tips

And if you can't find that person right away—let this book be a starting point.

Because sometimes, one conversation can do what months of preparation can't.

"I met a man who believed in me before I did.

And that belief became my breakthrough."

3.3. The Power of Self-Awareness

Before you can lead others, you must learn to lead yourself.

And that begins with one of the most underrated, yet powerful qualities an SSB aspirant can cultivate:

Self-awareness.

It's not taught in schools.

It's rarely emphasized in coaching institutes.

But in every SSB interview room, GTO task, and psychological test, it silently speaks on your behalf.

What is Self-Awareness, Really?

Self-awareness is the ability to understand:

- Who you are

- What you think

- Why you behave the way you do

- How you respond under pressure

- Where your strengths and blind spots lie

It is not about being perfect.

It's about being present—to your thoughts, your actions, your emotions, and your impact on others.

And in the Armed Forces, this trait is non-negotiable.

Because when you're leading men, making decisions in life-threatening situations, or standing accountable for your actions—you can't afford to be clueless about yourself.

My Turning Point: When I Looked Inward

After my rejections at Mysore and Allahabad, I made a mistake many make:

I started looking outward for reasons—format, interview panel, group dynamics, luck.

But nothing changed until I turned the question inward:

"What's stopping me from shining in that room?"

The answer wasn't in books. It was in my inner operating system.

I lacked fluency not because I didn't know English—but because I wasn't clear in my thinking.

I failed in group discussions not because others were louder—but because I didn't know what value I truly brought to the group.

I stumbled in interviews because I was trying to say the right things, not the *real* things.

And when I began to reflect honestly, everything shifted.

How Self-Awareness Shows Up at SSB

- In the WAT, when your instincts finish the sentence, not your strategy

- In the TAT, when the stories you write reveal your values

- In the SRT, when your reactions mirror your true temperament

- In the interview, when you're asked: *"What are your weaknesses?"* and you don't bluff

- In group tasks, where your behavior speaks louder than your words

You can't "prepare" for self-awareness the way you cram for a test.

You cultivate it—by asking deeper questions and listening without judgment.

Start With These Questions:

1. What are my three core values?

2. How do I react when I feel challenged, ignored, or under pressure?

3. What feedback have I received from others that made me uncomfortable—but true?

4. What situations bring out the best in me? The worst?

5.   What am I afraid people might discover about me? Why?

Write these down. Sit with them. The more honest your answers, the more powerful your growth.

The Officer's Edge: Clarity Within

The Armed Forces don't just want fit, fast, and fluent individuals.

They want people who are self-directed, emotionally balanced, and aware of who they are and what they stand for.

Because in the field, your decisions won't come from textbooks. They'll come from your character.

And your character is revealed in moments where no one is watching—but you are.

"The most dangerous soldier is the one who knows his enemy.

But the most powerful leader is the one who knows himself."

Before you win over the SSB, win over your inner chaos.

Understand yourself. Accept yourself. And then elevate yourself.

That's the kind of officer the nation needs.

Part II: Inside the SSB Mindset

Chapter 4

4. Understanding the SSB Ecosystem

If you think the SSB is just another interview, let me stop you right there.

The Service Selection Board (SSB) is not an exam you pass—it's an ecosystem that observes, challenges, and reveals who you truly are. It is one of the most unique and respected selection systems in the world. And understanding it is the first step to navigating it with clarity and confidence.

What is the SSB?

The SSB is a five-day selection process conducted by boards across India to assess candidates for commissioned officer roles in the Indian Armed Forces—Army, Navy, and Air Force. Unlike conventional exams that test only knowledge, the SSB is designed to evaluate personality, leadership, attitude, and emotional intelligence.

It's not just about *what you say or do.*

It's about *how you think, feel, and behave under pressure, in groups, and on your own.*

The Three-Dimensional Assessment

The SSB ecosystem rests on three pillars—each handled by a different assessor:

1. Psychologist

   o Sees *how you think when no one is watching*

   o Evaluates your subconscious patterns through tests like TAT, WAT, SRT, and Self-Description

2. GTO (Group Testing Officer)

   o Watches *how you behave in a team*

   o Assesses your interaction, initiative, physical courage, and cooperation during group tasks, obstacles, planning, and lecturette

3. Interviewing Officer (IO)

   o Gauges *how you respond one-on-one*

   o Looks at your self-awareness, decision-making, values, honesty, and officer-like mindset

These three assessors don't compare notes during the process. Each of them observes you from a different lens—but what they look for is consistent: Officer-Like Qualities (OLQs).

What Are OLQs (Officer-Like Qualities)?

These are the core traits that define a true leader in uniform. There are 15 officially listed OLQs, grouped under four key factors:

1. Planning & Organizing

- Effective Intelligence

- Reasoning Ability

- Organizing Ability

- Power of Expression

2. Social Adjustment

- Social Adaptability

- Cooperation

- Sense of Responsibility

3. Social Effectiveness

- Initiative

- Self-Confidence

- Speed of Decision

- Ability to Influence the Group

- Liveliness

4. Dynamic Personality

- Determination

- Courage

- Stamina

These qualities are not assessed by your *words alone*—they are drawn from your behavior, energy, and presence throughout the process.

The 5-Day Flow of the SSB

Day	Focus Area
Day 1	Screening – Verbal/Non-Verbal Test, PPDT (Picture Perception and Discussion Test)
Day 2	Psychology Tests – TAT, WAT, SRT, and Self-Description
Day 3 & 4	GTO Tasks & Personal Interview – Group Discussions, Planning, Obstacles, Lecturette, etc.
Day 5	Conference – Final board review and results declaration

Each day is crafted not to test your memory, but to observe your natural personality under different conditions.

Why This Matters

The SSB is not about passing a test—it's about showing the board that you already possess the traits they're looking for.

Which means the real preparation isn't about faking confidence or memorizing responses—it's about becoming more aware, adaptable, and authentic.

"The SSB doesn't ask you to be perfect.

It asks you to be real, responsible, and ready to grow."

To succeed in the SSB ecosystem:

- Understand the structure

- Respect the process

- Trust your preparation

- And most importantly—be yourself, at your best

Because when you stop trying to perform and start choosing to lead, the ecosystem recognizes the officer within you.

4.1. What is OLQ?

Every SSB aspirant hears this term again and again—OLQ. But what does it *really* mean?

OLQ stands for Officer-Like Qualities, the backbone of the entire SSB selection process. These are the traits and characteristics that define a capable, dependable, and inspiring leader in the Indian Armed Forces.

The SSB doesn't select you based on just knowledge or physical strength. It selects you because you naturally display these core qualities—in your thoughts, words, and actions.

"OLQs are not skills you perform. They are values you embody."

The 15 OLQs: A Closer Look

These are grouped into four major factors. Together, they form the foundation of a well-rounded officer.

Factor I: Planning & Organizing

Traits that reflect your intelligence and ability to handle tasks logically and clearly.

1. Effective Intelligence – Ability to grasp and solve practical problems.

2. Reasoning Ability – Logical thinking and clarity in judgment.

3. Organizing Ability – Planning resources, time, and people effectively.

4. Power of Expression – Communicating thoughts clearly, confidently, and concisely.

Factor II: Social Adjustment

Your ability to work and adjust within a group of people.

5. Social Adaptability – Adjusting easily with people from different backgrounds.

6. Cooperation – Willingness to work as part of a team.

7. Sense of Responsibility – Owning up to your duties and actions without excuses.

Factor III: Social Effectiveness

These qualities show how you influence and interact with people in high-stress or leadership situations.

8. Initiative – Taking action without being told.

9. Self-Confidence – Believing in yourself without arrogance.

10. Speed of Decision – Making timely and sound decisions.

11. Ability to Influence the Group – Leading others through ideas and behavior.

12. Liveliness – Positivity, enthusiasm, and energy in the face of challenges.

Factor IV: Dynamic Personality

Your inner strength and physical/mental stamina.

13. Determination – Never giving up, even under pressure.

14. Courage – Facing fear, danger, or hardship with calm and boldness.

15. Stamina – Endurance to handle physically and mentally demanding tasks.

Why OLQ Matters

OLQs are not checked in a single test. They're woven into every moment of your SSB:

- In your writing (Psych tests)

- In your talking (Interview & Group Discussion)

- In your doing (GTO tasks, Command Task, Obstacle Course)

- In your being (how you carry yourself across 5 days)

You can't fake OLQs. But you can develop and display them authentically—through self-awareness, reflection, and aligned action.

How to Build OLQs Naturally

- Take initiative in daily life

- Reflect on your decisions and reactions

- Lead without waiting for authority

- Improve communication and emotional balance

- Volunteer, take responsibility, help others

- Stay physically fit and mentally flexible

"OLQs are not for the SSB alone—they are for life.

Because once an officer, always an officer."

4.2. Myths and Facts About the SSB

The SSB is one of the most misunderstood selection processes in India. Over the years, countless myths have grown around it—shared in hostels, on YouTube, and across social media. While some may be well-intended, most of them misguide aspirants and create unnecessary pressure.

Let's bust some of the most common myths and replace them with facts—so you walk into the SSB with clarity, not confusion.

Myth 1: "You need to be fluent in English to get selected."

Fact: Language is only a medium, not a measure.

Yes, being clear in communication matters. But you don't have to speak polished English to succeed. You can express in Hindi or a mix—what matters more is how confidently and clearly you convey your thoughts.

Clarity beats fluency every time.

Myth 2: "Only extroverts and loud people get selected."

Fact: SSB doesn't reward volume—it values genuine leadership.

You don't need to dominate group discussions or shout instructions. Listening well, thinking clearly, and offering meaningful input matter much more than being the loudest voice in the room.

Introverts with substance are just as valuable as extroverts with style.

Myth 3: "You need to prepare perfect answers for the interview."

Fact: The interview is not a memory test. It's a personality assessment.

The IO wants to know *who you are*, not *what you've rehearsed*. Be honest, consistent, and self-aware. Fabricated stories or fake achievements can be easily spotted.

Authenticity always wins.

Myth 4: "You must complete all obstacles to get selected."

Fact: Physical performance is important, but it's not the only factor.

If you attempt obstacles with courage and energy—even if you don't finish all—your spirit and determination will still be noticed. More than completion, they're observing your mindset.

Grit over glory.

Myth 5: "A gap year or backlog will lead to rejection."

Fact: SSB is about potential, not perfection.

If you have valid reasons for academic delays or gaps—and you can explain them with maturity—it will not count against you. Your present attitude and clarity matter more than past slips.

Your story matters more than your score.

Myth 6: "If you cry or get emotional, you'll be seen as weak."

Fact: Officers are human too.

It's okay to feel. What matters is how you respond after. Emotional intelligence, resilience, and balance are key—not robotic calmness. The SSB values self-awareness and emotional maturity.

Courage includes vulnerability.

Myth 7: "Repeaters have no chance. They always select freshers."

Fact: Many candidates get selected after 2nd, 3rd, or even 5th attempts.

In fact, repeaters often have deeper self-awareness and clarity from past attempts. If you grow with each try, your chances only improve.

Persistence is a powerful officer-like quality.

Myth 8: "You must act like an officer to get selected."

Fact: You don't need to act—you need to become.

The SSB is not looking for pretenders. It looks for raw potential, natural leadership, and authentic personality traits. Don't copy others. Instead, develop the original version of yourself.

Don't perform. Transform.

Myth 9: "SSB is all about luck."

Fact: SSB is about alignment, not luck.

Yes, group dynamics vary. But the system is designed to observe individuals across multiple tasks and situations. If you're consistent, prepared, and self-aware, you'll stand out—regardless of the group.

Luck may open the door, but preparation walks you in.

Myth 10: "You need to be extraordinary to get selected."

Fact: You just need to be authentically you—with clarity, courage, and character.

Ordinary people with honest intentions, positive attitude, and balanced behavior make excellent officers. Don't aim to impress—aim to express your true self with confidence.

Being real is your biggest strength.

"In the SSB, myths confuse you.

Facts prepare you.

And self-awareness transforms you."

Don't be swayed by noise. Stay rooted in truth.

Because the more clearly you understand the process, the more confidently you can trust it.

4.3. The Five-Day Process: An Overview

The Service Selection Board (SSB) isn't just a test—it's a transformational experience. Over five carefully designed days, it evaluates not just your skills, but your thinking, behavior, leadership, emotional balance, and authenticity.

To succeed, you need to understand the flow. Once you know what to expect, you can walk into each day with clarity and confidence.

Here's a breakdown of the SSB's Five-Day Process:

Day 1: Screening – First Impressions Matter

Purpose: To filter out candidates who show the potential to be assessed further.

Components:

1. Intelligence Test (Verbal & Non-Verbal Reasoning)

- o   Quick problem-solving questions to test your basic mental sharpness.

2.   Picture Perception and Description Test (PPDT)

- o   A blurred image is shown for 30 seconds.

- o   You write a story based on your perception.

- o   Followed by narration and group discussion.

Key Focus: Observation, imagination, clarity of thought, and how well you express and collaborate.

Day 2: Psychology Tests – The Inner You

Purpose: To understand your subconscious mind and natural personality.

Components:

1.   Thematic Apperception Test (TAT)

- o   11 picture slides + 1 blank.

- o   Write short stories that reflect your thinking style.

2.   Word Association Test (WAT)

- o   60 words shown for 15 seconds each.

- o   Write the first sentence that comes to mind.

3. Situation Reaction Test (SRT)

   o   60 real-life scenarios in 30 minutes.

   o   Write your reactions quickly and practically.

4. Self-Description (SD)

   o   Write how you're perceived by parents, friends, teachers, and yourself.

Key Focus: Thought clarity, values, emotional maturity, and consistency across responses.

Day 3 & 4: GTO Tasks & Interview – The Action Begins

Purpose: To assess your group dynamics, physical courage, leadership, and communication.

Group Testing Officer (GTO) Tasks:

- Group Discussions (GD)

- Group Planning Exercise (GPE)

- Progressive Group Task (PGT)

- Group Obstacle Race (GOR)

- Half Group Task (HGT)

- Lecturette

- Command Task (CT)

- Individual Obstacles (IO)

- Final Group Task (FGT)

Key Focus: Leadership, cooperation, initiative, physical ability, and your contribution in a group setting.

Personal Interview:

- Usually conducted on Day 2, 3, or 4, depending on scheduling.

- One-on-one session with the Interviewing Officer.

- Questions based on your PIQ (Personal Information Questionnaire), academics, hobbies, current affairs, personal values, and decision-making.

Key Focus: Clarity, honesty, decision-making ability, and overall officer-like personality.

Day 5: Conference – The Final Verdict

Purpose: All assessors come together to review your overall performance.

- A formal setting where all candidates are called in, one by one.

- The Board may ask 1–2 light questions or a situational question.

- It's more of a final review and confirmation of assessment.

Key Focus: Consistency across the 3 dimensions—Psychology, GTO, and Interview.

After all candidates have been seen, results are announced. Those recommended are kept back for medical examinations, while the rest are bid farewell with encouragement for future attempts.

What Makes the Process Unique?

- It's holistic—measuring mind, body, and behavior.

- It's non-competitive—you're evaluated individually, not against others.

- It's fair—assessors are trained to spot potential, not perfection.

- It's introspective—you discover a lot about yourself in the process.

"The SSB doesn't just test you—it reflects you.

And in that reflection, you find both your strengths and your story."

Prepare not just to clear each day, but to evolve with each step.

Chapter 5

5. THE PSYCHOLOGY BEHIND SELECTION

If you've ever wondered why the SSB selection process is so different from any other competitive exam, the answer lies in one word:

Psychology.

Unlike conventional tests that focus on what you know, the SSB is designed to reveal who you are. It doesn't just check your memory or marks—it evaluates your mindset, motivation, and maturity.

And that's why understanding the psychology behind selection is your greatest advantage.

The Core Idea: Selection, Not Elimination

Let's begin by clearing a major misconception.

The SSB is not designed to "filter out" candidates. It's designed to discover potential officers—those who naturally exhibit Officer-Like Qualities (OLQs) in their thinking, responses, behavior, and choices.

You're not being tested to *eliminate* you.

You're being observed to *understand* you.

Why Psychology Matters More Than Preparation

The psychological tests at SSB—TAT, WAT, SRT, and Self-Description—aren't about right or wrong answers. There is no "model response." These tests are structured to uncover your natural personality—your instincts, beliefs, values, and emotional intelligence.

Why?

Because in the Armed Forces:

- Decisions are made under pressure.

- You must lead without rehearsal.

- Your mindset matters more than your memory.

That's why selection boards want to know:

"Can this person handle uncertainty, responsibility, and leadership with balance and courage?"

What the Assessors Are Really Looking For

1. Consistency – Are your thoughts, behavior, and personality traits aligned across all tests?

2. Authenticity – Are your responses genuine, or are you trying to impress?

3. Self-Awareness – Do you understand your strengths and limitations honestly?

4. Emotional Stability – Can you handle failure, criticism, pressure, and teamwork with maturity?

5. Social Effectiveness – Can you influence, listen, speak, and cooperate in a group?

6. Leadership by Nature – Do you take initiative naturally, or only when prompted?

Why Fake Responses Fail

Many aspirants try to memorize "model stories," "ideal word associations," or "perfect SRT replies."

But here's the problem:

Psychologists don't judge your answers in isolation—they look for patterns across everything you say and do.

If your TAT stories say you're brave, but your WAT responses show fear and your SRT reactions show indecision—there's a mismatch.

That inconsistency sends up a red flag.

"You don't get selected for sounding like an officer.

You get selected for thinking, behaving, and responding like one."

How to Align with the Psychology of Selection

1. Know Yourself – Regularly reflect on your decisions, reactions, strengths, and areas of growth.

2. Be Honest – Fake confidence is easy to detect. Show real self-belief, even if imperfect.

3. Think Clearly – Practice clarity of thought, not just fluency of speech.

4. Respond Naturally – Don't pause to "create the perfect line." Say what you feel, guided by purpose.

5. Develop Daily Discipline – Your responses in tests will mirror your real-life choices and behavior.

Psychological Fitness is Trainable

Just like physical strength, mental clarity and emotional balance can be developed.

And the best part? You don't need expensive coaching to do it.

You need:

- Honest reflection

- Structured journaling

- Real conversations

- Service-oriented thinking

- Daily improvement in communication and responsibility

"At SSB, you're not just being tested.

You're being revealed—to the Board, and to yourself."

So don't try to hack the system.

Grow into the kind of person the system naturally selects.

That's the true psychology behind SSB success.

5.1. How the Mind is Evaluated

At the SSB, your mind is under the microscope—but not in the way you might expect.

They're not looking for how much theory you've memorized or how smart you sound.

They want to see how you think, feel, react, decide, and express—especially under pressure.

This is what makes the SSB so unique and deeply psychological.

The entire process is structured to evaluate your mental wiring, your emotional maturity, and your natural personality—not just your performance.

Let's break it down.

1. Through Thought: TAT, WAT, and SRT

The psychologist's job is to get past your surface-level behavior and understand what's happening inside your mind. They do this through structured tests that leave very little time to think, filter, or fake.

Thematic Apperception Test (TAT)

You're shown a picture for 30 seconds, and then you must write a story in 4 minutes.

What they observe:

- What kind of characters you create

- How you approach problems

- Whether your stories reflect optimism, courage, and responsibility

- Your emotional tone—positive, balanced, or extreme

Word Association Test (WAT)

You see 60 words—one every 15 seconds—and write the first sentence that comes to mind.

What they observe:

- Your instinctive thoughts and associations

- Positivity vs negativity

- Social concern, leadership attitude, and mental flexibility

Situation Reaction Test (SRT)

You're given 60 real-life situations in 30 minutes. You must write how you would respond.

What they observe:

- Decision-making speed and clarity

- Practicality and presence of mind

- Responsibility, self-control, and empathy

- Whether your solutions are impulsive or thoughtful

2. Through Self-Reflection: The Self-Description Test (SDT)

In this task, you describe yourself through the eyes of others—your parents, friends, teachers—and then in your own words.

What they observe:

- Your level of self-awareness

- Whether you know your strengths and weaknesses

- If there's alignment between how you think you are and how others see you

- Your willingness to grow and improve

This test helps the psychologist understand your emotional intelligence and authenticity. It's not about being perfect. It's about being honest and open.

3. Through Behavior: GTO & Interview Tasks

Although these tasks are not handled by the psychologist, they provide real-time proof of your mental traits.

For example:

- Do you get nervous or stay calm under pressure?

- Are your actions aligned with your beliefs?

- Can you express ideas clearly and take others along?

- Do you bounce back after mistakes or give up?

The consistency between your psychology tests and your group performance is key.

If you show leadership in your stories but shrink back in group tasks—there's a mismatch.

"Your mind speaks louder than your mouth.

And the SSB listens closely."

What the Mind Evaluation Reveals

They aren't judging your life story—they're studying your:

- Patterns of thinking

- Ability to prioritize and take initiative

- Handling of fear, failure, or criticism

- Level of maturity, empathy, and courage

- True Officer-Like Qualities (OLQs) embedded in your personality

The Real Secret: It's Not About 'Cracking' the Tests

The SSB doesn't want scripted answers. They want natural, thoughtful, authentic people who are trainable, balanced, and clear-minded.

So, if you're wondering how the mind is evaluated—here's the answer:

They evaluate how aligned you are within yourself—thoughts, words, and actions.

Tips to Prepare Mentally (Not Memorize)

- Journal daily – Reflect on your day, thoughts, and reactions

- Read real stories – Build maturity through life examples

- Stay updated – Awareness of world events builds critical thinking

- Practice clarity – Answer "why" for every choice you make

- Be honest with yourself – Growth starts with real self-talk

"You don't need a brilliant mind. You need a balanced one."

Because in the Armed Forces, it's not about being perfect. It's about being prepared, present, and purposeful.

5.2. Authenticity vs Memorization

There are two kinds of aspirants who walk into the SSB.

One walks in with memorized answers, polished lines, and model stories borrowed from books, blogs, or coaching classes.

The other walks in with clarity of thought, honest experiences, and the courage to express who they really are.

Guess who gets selected?

The one who is real—not rehearsed.

In the SSB, authenticity isn't optional. It's essential.

You're not judged for being imperfect. You're judged for being inconsistent, artificial, or unsure of your own identity.

The Trap of Memorization

Many aspirants fall into the trap of:

- Copy-pasting stories for TAT

- Memorizing "power words" for WAT

- Preparing ideal answers for SRT

- Writing what sounds good in the Self-Description

Why?

Because they believe there's a "right answer" to every situation.

But the SSB isn't about right answers. It's about honest responses.

When you memorize, you:

- Lose spontaneity

- Sound artificial

- Struggle under pressure

- Break down when the situation changes

- Create contradictions across tests

And the assessors? They're trained to spot fakeness in seconds.

"A fake story may pass a test. But it cannot pass the truth check of your own personality."

Why Authenticity Always Wins

Authenticity means:

- Expressing what you truly believe, not what you think they want to hear

- Accepting your flaws without shame

- Speaking from real experiences

- Showing up with natural energy—not forced enthusiasm

Authentic aspirants:

- Speak with clarity and consistency

- Handle unexpected questions with calmness

- Show stable behavior across all tasks

- Leave a lasting impression—because real always stands out

Memorization Fails in These Areas Most

Test	Common Memorized Mistakes	What the Board Looks For
TAT	Copied hero-centric stories	Realistic, socially meaningful stories with initiative
WAT	Idealistic, robotic phrases	Natural, emotionally aware sentences
SRT	Over-ideal, impractical responses	Quick, balanced, responsible decisions
Interview	Scripted answers, fake achievements	Honest, aligned personality reflection
Self-Description	Lines learned from the internet	Honest self-perception with a growth mindset

How to Cultivate Authenticity

1. Journal your own stories – Write 10 real-life experiences where you showed leadership, responsibility, or clarity.

2. Answer "why" to your choices – Build self-awareness about your decisions and opinions.

3. Practice, but don't script – Rehearse speaking, not memorizing.

4. Accept your flaws – Confidence comes from ownership, not perfection.

5. Ask: "If I had no one to impress, how would I answer this?"

In the SSB, Authenticity Sounds Like:

- "Sir, I haven't read many books, but I enjoy observing people and learning from conversations."

- "Yes, I've failed before—but I used that phase to understand myself better."

- "I'm working on my hesitation in group settings. That's why I've taken up small leadership roles in college."

- "This story is from my life—I've been in a similar situation, and here's what I did…"

"Truth, even when imperfect, carries more weight than a polished lie."

"Don't try to be the perfect candidate.

Be the real you—with clarity, courage, and a commitment to grow."

Because in the Armed Forces, they don't select actors.

They select leaders—and leadership begins with authenticity.

5.3. From Nervousness to Naturalness

Almost every SSB aspirant begins their journey with a few common companions:

Shaky hands, racing thoughts, and the fear of being judged.

It's completely natural. After all, you're walking into a high-stakes environment, competing for one of the most respected roles in the country.

But here's the truth you need to remember:

"The SSB doesn't expect you to be fearless.

It expects you to rise despite the fear—and respond with calm clarity."

This is the journey from nervousness to naturalness—and every officer has walked it.

Where Nervousness Comes From

Let's break it down. Nervousness is often born from:

- The pressure to "crack" the SSB

- Fear of being judged or compared

- Doubts about your own capabilities

- Overthinking every action or word

- Past failures or the "what if I fail again?" mindset

And guess what?

Everyone feels this. Even the best aspirants. Even those who eventually get recommended.

The difference is—they learn how to manage it and let their natural self emerge.

Naturalness: What the SSB Actually Looks For

Naturalness doesn't mean being casual or careless.

It means being present, composed, and aligned with your real thoughts and actions.

Natural aspirants:

- Speak honestly, without trying to impress

- Think clearly, even under pressure

- Smile, pause, and breathe when they need to

- Make mistakes—but recover with grace

- Come across as grounded, not robotic

"When you stop trying to perform, and just choose to participate fully—you become natural."

How to Move From Nervousness to Naturalness

1. Prepare, But Don't Pretend

Know your strengths, your stories, your views. But don't script them. Speak from lived experience.

2. Practice Exposure

Speak in front of a mirror, in front of friends, record yourself. The more you expose yourself to real conditions, the less power fear has.

3. Breathe and Slow Down

Before any task or interview, take 3 deep breaths. It signals safety to your nervous system and brings calm to your voice.

4. Accept the First 10 Seconds

The first 10 seconds are always the most nervous. Let them pass. Don't fight them—breathe through them.

5. Focus on the Task, Not the Result

You can't control the outcome, but you can control your presence in the moment. Pour yourself into the activity—let the result take care of itself.

What Naturalness Looks Like in SSB

- Telling a story in TAT that's not perfect, but heartfelt

- Smiling when you forget a point during Lecturette, and picking up again

- Saying "I'm not sure, but here's what I think..." in an interview

- Listening fully during GD before adding your point

- Pausing during WAT when stuck—but writing what's true for you

Confidence Isn't Loud. It's Aligned.

When your thoughts, words, and behavior are aligned, you feel calm.

You don't need to *act* confident. You simply become confident.

And that's what the SSB wants—not a candidate with zero nervousness, but a leader who stays steady in spite of it.

"Your nervousness is not a weakness. It's a sign that you care.

But beyond that nervousness lies your true strength—

The ability to stay natural, no matter how unnatural the environment feels."

So breathe. Ground yourself.

You don't have to be perfect. You just have to be present and real.

That's what makes you officer material.

Chapter 6

6. CLARITY, CHARACTER & COMMUNICATION

The Three Invisible Forces That Define an Officer

When you walk into the SSB, you won't be asked:

"Do you have clarity?"

"Is your character strong?"

"How well do you communicate?"

But trust me, these three traits will silently define everything you say, do, and become in those five days.

They are not written on any test paper.

But they are written all over your presence.

Let's explore how these three pillars—Clarity, Character, and Communication—work together to shape not only your SSB performance, but your future as a leader.

Clarity: The Power of Knowing Who You Are and What You Stand For

Clarity is not just about knowledge.

It's about knowing yourself:

- What are your strengths and weaknesses?

- What do you believe in?

- Why do you want to join the Armed Forces?

- How do you make decisions?

An aspirant with clarity:

- Answers questions confidently—even when unsure

- Writes stories with purpose, not just drama

- Gives reasons behind actions in the SRT

- Explains career choices in the interview without confusion

"When your mind is clear, your actions follow with confidence."

At SSB, clarity leads to calmness, and calmness leads to credibility.

Character: The Inner Compass That Guides You When No One is Watching

Character isn't something you can fake. It's not a line on your PIQ.

It shows up in:

- How you treat your group mates

- Whether you speak the truth, even when uncomfortable

- Whether you stay honest in your stories and interviews

- How you handle feedback, pressure, or even small setbacks

An aspirant with character:

- Doesn't blame others when things go wrong

- Admits gaps with humility

- Stands by their principles without arrogance

- Shows integrity in words and actions

"The SSB doesn't just look for intelligence. It looks for integrity."

Because in the real world, officers are trusted with lives—not just files.

Communication: The Bridge Between Your Mind and the Mission

Communication isn't just about fluency. It's about impact.

Can you express your ideas clearly, calmly, and confidently—whether in writing, speaking, or action?

In the SSB, your communication is visible in:

- Your narration and GD during PPDT

- Your stories and sentences during psych tests

- Your explanations during GTO tasks

- Your responses in the interview

- Your Lecturette delivery

An effective communicator:

- Keeps it simple, but powerful

- Speaks with presence, not pressure

- Listens first, then contributes

- Uses body language wisely—eye contact, posture, tone

"Great communication is not about big words. It's about big clarity."

Together, They Make You Unshakeable

Trait	What it Builds	How it Shows at SSB
Clarity	Confidence & calm	Structured responses, clear ideas
Character	Integrity & trust	Consistency across tests, humility
Communication	Leadership & influence	Effective expression, presence

You may forget model answers. You may miss one obstacle.

But if you carry clarity, character, and communication, the board will see someone ready to lead.

"You don't need to shout to be heard.

You don't need to fake to be selected.

You just need to be clear, real, and impactful."

Let these three become your core training—before, during, and after SSB.

Because even after you wear the uniform, they will remain your greatest assets.

6.1. Building Your Inner Officer

Before the Stars on Your Shoulder, Earn the Strength in Your Soul

Becoming an officer doesn't start with the SSB.

It begins long before that—in the quiet decisions you make daily, the discipline you build within, and the values you choose to live by.

It starts with building your inner officer.

Because the SSB doesn't select people based on tricks, tips, or temporary performance.

It selects those who already carry the spirit of service, leadership, and responsibility—not just on paper, but in their personality.

Who Is the Inner Officer?

The *Inner Officer* is the part of you that:

- Thinks clearly under pressure

- Stands by your values even when no one is watching

- Rises when others hesitate

- Listens with empathy and speaks with impact

- Reflects deeply, acts deliberately, and serves selflessly

It is not a role. It's a state of being. And it's built through small, daily choices.

Steps to Build Your Inner Officer

1. Live With Purpose

Ask yourself:

"Why do I want to join the Armed Forces?"

Go beyond surface-level answers. When your *why* is clear, your energy and focus sharpen. Officers don't live for applause—they live for purpose.

2. Practice Daily Discipline

You don't need a parade ground to train. You can start at home:

- Wake up with intention

- Set daily goals

- Keep your promises to yourself

- Show up on time—even if no one else is watching

"Discipline is not control. It's self-respect in action."

3. Make Decisions with Integrity

When faced with a choice, ask:

"What would an officer do here?"

Choose honesty over shortcuts. Choose calm over panic. Choose responsibility over blame. Even small actions build your ethical foundation.

4. Lead Where You Are

You don't need a uniform to lead. Start where you are:

- Take initiative in your college or community

- Help teammates succeed

- Stand up for what's right, even if it's uncomfortable

- Leadership is not a title. It's an action.

5. Build Emotional Resilience

Life won't always go your way. Rejections, setbacks, failures—they're all part of your journey.

An officer learns not just to endure them, but to grow through them.

Breathe. Reflect. Reset.

"You don't rise by avoiding storms. You rise by facing them."

6. Serve Before You're Selected

Look around. Who can you help?

How can you contribute?

Service is not something that begins after joining the forces. It begins the moment you start thinking like a protector and contributor.

Remember: SSB Doesn't Create Officers—It Recognizes Them

You don't "become" an officer at the end of training.

You start becoming one the moment you commit to building yourself with integrity, intention, and inner clarity.

And when you carry that energy into the SSB, something shifts.

You no longer walk in as an "aspirant."

You walk in as someone who's already walking the talk of leadership.

"The uniform is earned by those who've already worn the officer's mindset within."

So build that mindset. Strengthen your values.

Speak with clarity. Lead with humility. Serve with courage.

Because long before they pin stars on your shoulder,

they will see the spark in your soul.

6.2. Importance of Verbal and Non-Verbal Expression

Because How You Say It Matters Just as Much as What You Say

In the Armed Forces, communication can save lives, build trust, and lead teams into the unknown.

And at the SSB, your ability to express yourself—both verbally and non-verbally—is under constant observation.

This isn't about being loud or stylish.

It's about being clear, confident, composed, and credible.

Because communication isn't just a skill. For an officer, it's a strategic tool.

Verbal Expression: Speak Like a Leader, Not a Parrot

Your words matter—not just what you say, but *how* you say it.

In the SSB, verbal expression is observed during:

- Narration (PPDT)

- Group Discussions (GD)

- Lecturette

- Interview

- Command Task (GTO)

- Even casual conversations during your stay!

What they look for:

- Clarity – Do you express your ideas logically and simply?

- Confidence – Do you speak with self-assurance, without arrogance?

- Tone & Modulation – Can you engage without shouting?

- Relevance – Are your inputs meaningful, or just fillers?

- Brevity – Can you say more in fewer words?

"Verbal communication is not about impressing. It's about influencing with intent and respect."

Non-Verbal Expression: When Your Body Speaks Before You Do

Before you even open your mouth, your posture, expressions, and gestures already speak volumes.

In the SSB, your non-verbal cues are constantly noted:

- During tasks

- In the interview waiting area

- While listening to others

- Even while walking, sitting, or greeting officers

Key non-verbal signals they observe:

- Posture – Stand and sit straight. It shows confidence and readiness.

- Eye Contact – Shows honesty and attentiveness (not staring, but steady).

- Facial Expression – Balanced; neither tense nor over-expressive.

- Gestures – Natural and controlled—not over-animated.

- Energy – Calm, engaged, and grounded body language.

"Your body cannot lie—so make sure your actions reflect your values."

Why Both Matter Together

Words without the right energy seem fake.

And confidence without clarity feels empty.

When your verbal and non-verbal expressions align, you project:

- Authenticity

- Leadership presence

- Respect and confidence

- Emotional intelligence

This is especially important in:

- The Interview Room – where your truth must meet poise

- The Group Discussion – where your opinion must not overpower respect

- The Command Task – where instructions must be clear and body language firm

- The Conference – where a simple greeting can carry authority

Tips to Improve Expression

For Verbal:

- Practice speaking on everyday topics (use the "Lecturette format")

- Record yourself and review tone, clarity, and structure

- Read aloud to improve pronunciation and modulation

- Engage in real conversations—not just SSB rehearsals

For Non-Verbal:

- Observe your own posture and gestures in the mirror

- Slow down your movements—relax your shoulders, open your stance

- Maintain a natural, gentle smile

- Walk with calmness and purpose

- Practice greeting with firm eye contact and confidence

"An officer doesn't just speak well—they express with presence, calm, and clarity."

So train your words to reflect your mind.

Train your body to reflect your truth.

And together, they'll reflect the officer within.

6.3. Developing Leadership Presence

Because Officers Are Not Just Heard—They're Felt, Seen, and Followed

At the SSB—and later, in uniform—you're not selected just for your ability to lead. You're selected for your ability to inspire others to follow.

That ability comes from one invisible but undeniable force:

Leadership Presence.

It's not about rank.

It's not about loudness.

It's not even about being the smartest in the room.

Leadership presence is the quiet confidence, energy, and authenticity that makes others pay attention when you enter a space or speak up in a group.

What Is Leadership Presence?

It's the impact of your presence, not your performance.

It's when your:

- Thoughts carry clarity

- Words carry weight

- Body carries composure

- Energy carries purpose

People feel it. Assessors notice it.

And in the SSB, it sets you apart without you having to "stand out."

"Presence is not how many people you lead—it's how powerfully you lead yourself."

How Leadership Presence Shows Up at SSB

Situation	Leadership Presence Looks Like
Group Discussions	Speaking with calm confidence, listening actively, summarizing wisely
GTO Tasks	Helping teammates, taking initiative naturally, showing responsibility
Command Task	Giving clear instructions, encouraging others, staying composed under scrutiny
Interview	Owning your story, answering honestly, staying calm under curveballs
Lecturette	Speaking with structured thought, eye contact, and steady voice
Day-to-Day Behavior	Discipline, respect, cheerfulness, and consistency—even outside tasks

How to Build Your Leadership Presence

1. Be Centered, Not Scattered

Before you lead others, you must be rooted in yourself.

Practice self-awareness, mindfulness, and emotional balance.

Calmness is powerful.

2. Speak With Clarity and Intent

Think before you speak. Use fewer, stronger words. Don't speak just to fill the silence—speak to add value.

"When your thoughts are clear, your voice becomes strong—even if soft."

3. Stand Like a Leader

Your body speaks before you do:

- Keep your posture upright

- Walk with purpose

- Use open hand gestures

- Smile gently, not forcefully

- Hold eye contact with warmth and confidence

4. Be the One Who Uplifts Others

Leadership presence is not about dominating. It's about creating psychological safety for others.

Encourage. Include. Stay grounded. Be humble but firm.

5. Consistency Builds Credibility

True presence comes from showing up with the same energy, integrity, and commitment—across every task, every moment. Even when no one's watching.

Ask Yourself Daily:

- Do people feel safe and encouraged when I speak?

- Do I listen deeply, or just wait for my turn to talk?

- Do I carry calmness into chaos, or add to the noise?

- Does my energy reflect purpose—or performance?

"A leader isn't the loudest in the room.

They're the one everyone looks to—when things get quiet."

You don't need to fake authority.

You need to live with authenticity.

And that will create the kind of presence that earns trust, inspires action, and commands respect.

Start building your inner leader today—so that by the time you reach the SSB, your presence speaks before you do.

PART III: DAY-BY-DAY SSB DECODED

Chapter 7

7. Day 1: Screening Test & First Impressions

Because How You Start Often Sets the Tone for the Journey

Your first day at the SSB is like the opening scene of a powerful film—and you're both the actor and the director.

The screening process determines whether you stay for the next four days or head back home the same evening. It's a high-pressure filter. But if you understand it—and show up with clarity, calmness, and confidence—it becomes your gateway to success.

Let's break it down:

What Is the Screening Test?

The screening process is designed to evaluate:

- Your mental sharpness (through reasoning tests)

- Your observational ability and imagination (through PPDT)

- Your communication and group behavior (through narration and discussion)

Only 30–40% of candidates typically get screened in, so making a strong first impression is key.

Step 1: Intelligence Test (Verbal & Non-Verbal Reasoning)

You'll be given two sets of multiple-choice tests, usually consisting of:

- Series completion

- Coding-decoding

- Analogies

- Visual puzzles

- Pattern recognition

Time: 17–25 minutes per set

Goal: Clear mental processing, speed, and accuracy

Tips:

- Practice beforehand using standard reasoning books

- Manage time—don't get stuck on tough ones

- Read questions carefully

- Don't guess randomly

"Think clearly. Act quickly. Trust your instincts."

Step 2: Picture Perception and Description Test (PPDT)

You will be shown a hazy picture for 30 seconds.

Then, you'll have 4 minutes to write a story based on what you perceive.

You must note:

- No. of characters

- Age, gender, mood

- What led to the situation

- What's happening now

- What will be the outcome

Your story should be logical, realistic, and ideally showcase leadership, responsibility, and optimism.

Tips:

- Don't overthink the story—keep it simple and meaningful

- Avoid heroic fantasies—be relatable and socially aware

- Make the main character reflect *you*

- Focus on thought process, not fancy language

Step 3: Narration and Group Discussion

Once stories are written, you'll be grouped (typically 10–15 candidates).

Each of you will narrate your story in one minute, followed by an open group discussion to arrive at a common story.

Narration Tips:

- Be confident, clear, and loud enough

- Maintain a steady tone—no rushing

- Eye contact with the group, not the officer

- No paper reading—rely on memory

Discussion Tips:

- Don't dominate or interrupt

- Contribute meaningfully—listen, build on others' points

- If chaos happens, stay calm and be the voice of reason

- If group agrees, be the one to summarize clearly

"You're not just being judged for what you say—but how you behave when others speak."

What Assessors Observe on Day 1

Area	What They're Watching
Intelligence	Logical thinking under time pressure
Story Writing	Creativity, clarity, and leadership orientation
Narration	Confidence, articulation, presence
Group Discussion	Initiative, cooperation, listening, calmness under pressure
Overall Demeanor	First impression, energy, discipline, grooming

Come Prepared:

- Arrive a day early if possible—rest well

- Wear clean, formal clothes (light shirt, dark trousers, polished shoes)

- Groom neatly—hair, shave, nails

- Carry your documents, photos, pens, and stationery

- Most importantly—carry your composure and conviction

"The Screening Test isn't about perfection. It's about projection—

How well you project clarity, courage, and calmness in your thoughts and actions."

So walk in with purpose.

Sit with confidence.

Speak with clarity.

And let your presence tell the board:

"I am officer material—and I'm here to show you why."

7.1. Intelligence Test (Verbal & Non-Verbal)

Your First Mental Mission at the SSB

The Intelligence Test is your first task on Day 1 of the SSB—and often your first impression on the assessors.

It's not a test of your academic knowledge, but of your mental agility, decision-making speed, and logical reasoning.

Think of it as the SSB's way of asking:

"Can you think clearly and act quickly under pressure?"

Let's break it down so you're not just ready—but strategically prepared.

What Is the Intelligence Test?

The Intelligence Test at SSB is divided into two parts:

1. Verbal Reasoning – Tests how well you handle information through words, numbers, and logic

2. Non-Verbal Reasoning – Tests your ability to interpret visual patterns and symbols without using language

Each part typically has 40–50 questions, and you'll have around 17–25 minutes to solve them.

Verbal Reasoning

This section evaluates how well you understand patterns, relationships, and logic through language and numbers.

Common Question Types:

- Series Completion (e.g. 2, 4, 8, 16, ?)

- Coding-Decoding (e.g. If CAT = 24, then DOG = ?)

- Blood Relations (e.g. "A is the son of B's sister...")

- Directions & Distances (e.g. "Ram walks 5m north...")

- Number and Alphabet Analogy

- Logical Deductions and Syllogisms

- Odd One Out

- Statement & Conclusion / Cause-Effect

Tips:

- Practice common patterns beforehand

- Don't try to solve by gut feeling—apply logic

- Skip lengthy or confusing questions; time is limited

- Keep calm—panicking affects processing speed

Non-Verbal Reasoning

This section tests your visual intelligence—the ability to recognize sequences, shapes, and symmetry.

Common Question Types:

- Series of Shapes

- Mirror and Water Images

- Odd Figure Out

- Pattern Completion

- Embedded Figures

- Cube Folding & Paper Cutting

You'll be shown figures, diagrams, or image sequences—and must identify the correct option that continues or completes the pattern.

Tips:

- Focus on direction, rotation, shape size, and shading

- Practice "figure series" puzzles to build speed

- Train your eyes, not just your brain—it's about visual recognition

- Don't overthink—your first instinct is often correct

Time Management is Key

You'll likely have less than 30 seconds per question.

That means:

- Answer what you know quickly

- Skip what slows you down

- Don't leave the sheet blank—guess intelligently in the last few seconds if needed (no negative marking)

"In this test, speed + accuracy = screening success."

How to Prepare Effectively

- Use standard books on *Verbal & Non-Verbal Reasoning*

- Solve previous SSB-level intelligence questions

- Practice daily for at least 15–20 minutes

- Time your mock tests—simulate real conditions

- Focus more on visual reasoning if that's your weak spot

What the Assessors Look For

They want to see:

- Sharp thinking

- Calm under pressure

- Logical analysis

- Focused attention

- Basic problem-solving skills

Even though this part may seem mechanical, it tells them a lot about your mental readiness for the high-stress, fast-paced environment of military life.

"In the Intelligence Test, you don't need to be a genius.

You just need to be quick, clear, and calm."

So sharpen your thinking.

Practice with focus.

And remember—this is just the first step on your journey to becoming officer material.

7.2. Picture Perception & Description Test (PPDT)

Your First Real Test of Perception, Clarity, and Expression

The PPDT is one of the most crucial tasks on Day 1 of the SSB.

Why? Because it tests how you observe, how you think, how you write, and how you speak—all in just a few minutes.

In fact, many candidates get screened out not because of weak reasoning, but because they fail to express a clear, logical, and purposeful story in the PPDT.

Let's understand this test deeply—so you don't just pass it, but make a lasting first impression.

What Is PPDT?

PPDT = Picture Perception + Description + Discussion

You'll be shown a blurred or ambiguous picture for 30 seconds.

Then, you'll get 4 minutes to write a story based on it.

After that:

- You will narrate your story individually (1 minute)

- Then take part in a group discussion to form a common story

Purpose of the Test

The assessors want to know:

- Can you observe details quickly and accurately?

- Can you process a situation logically and form a coherent response?

- Can you express your thoughts clearly and confidently?

- Can you work with others in a group setting?

"In PPDT, they are not testing your English—they are observing your energy, clarity, and mindset."

Part 1: Writing the Story (4 minutes)

Here's what you must do:

First 30 Seconds – Perception Phase

- Observe the picture carefully

- Identify number of characters, their age, gender, and mood (happy/sad/neutral)

- Note what the scene suggests (rural/urban, indoors/outdoors, peaceful/action)

Next 4 Minutes – Write the Story

Use this simple 3-part structure:

1. What led to the situation?

2. What is happening now?

3. What will be the outcome?

Make your main character proactive and positive, and ideally, reflect your own personality.

Tips for Writing:

- Be realistic—not filmy

- Show leadership, problem-solving, and initiative

- Avoid violence or extreme drama

- Keep grammar simple—clarity matters more than complexity

- Use present or past tense consistently

Part 2: Narration (1 Minute)

You will be called one by one to narrate your story. This is a vital moment to showcase your presence and clarity.

Narration Format:

"Good morning, gentlemen.

There are 3 characters in my story—2 males aged 25 and 40, and 1 female aged 22. The mood of all characters is positive.

The central character is Rohan, a 25-year-old software engineer... *(continue your story)*"

Tips for Narration:

- Speak with calm confidence

- Don't memorize—speak naturally based on what you wrote

- Maintain eye contact with the group, not with the officer

- Speak at a moderate pace—not rushed, not sluggish

- Sit straight, avoid fidgeting

"Narration is not a performance—it's a reflection of your mindset under pressure."

Part 3: Group Discussion (GD)

After everyone narrates, the group (10–15 candidates) will have a free-flowing discussion to form a common story.

This is where many get filtered out—not for what they say, but how they behave.

In GD, Show:

- Respectful communication

- Active listening

- Logical reasoning

- Team spirit

- Calm leadership (not aggression)

If the group gets chaotic, be the voice of reason:

"Let's hear him out first."

"Why don't we build on that point?"

"We all seem to agree on the central theme—let's move forward."

"The officer-like quality here is not dominance. It's diplomacy under pressure."

What the Assessors Look For in PPDT:

Phase	Qualities Observed
Writing	Clarity, logic, originality, OLQs reflected in the story
Narration	Confidence, structure, fluency, presence of mind
GD	Teamwork, communication, leadership, attitude, maturity

Common Mistakes to Avoid:

- Writing unrealistic or dramatic stories

- Copying stories from coaching or YouTube

- Trying to "win" the GD instead of contributing

- Speaking too much or not speaking at all

- Arguing, interrupting, or being aggressive

"PPDT isn't about finding the best story.

It's about showing the best version of your thinking, expression, and collaboration."

Be calm.

Be clear.

Be constructive.

And let the story you tell—on paper and in presence—show them who you really are.

7.3. Tips for Narration and Group Discussion (GD)

Stand Out Without Shouting. Lead Without Dominating.

Narration and GD are often where SSB aspirants either shine—or silently get screened out.

They are not just about how much you speak, but how well you think, express, and engage in a group setting.

This phase tests your clarity of thought, communication skills, group behavior, and officer-like mindset—all in a matter of minutes.

Let's break it down and give you smart, effective tips to bring out your best.

Narration Tips: One Minute That Matters

1. Structure Your Narration

Follow this proven format:

Number of characters, gender, age, mood

What led to the situation

What is happening now

What will be the outcome

It creates a flow and shows you are organized in thought.

2. Be Clear and Concise

- Don't ramble. Stick to the point.

- Speak slowly enough to be understood, but not so slow that you lose energy.

- Use short, strong sentences. Avoid long-winded storytelling.

3. Speak With Confidence, Not Arrogance

- Sit upright with a calm but alert posture

- Make steady eye contact with the group, not the assessors

- Avoid filler words like "uh," "like," "basically..."

- Don't read from memory—recreate the story naturally

4. Finish Within Time

Your narration must be under 1 minute. Practice timed delivery during prep.

Going over time shows poor planning and lack of control.

"Narration is not a performance—it's a demonstration of clarity and control under pressure."

Group Discussion Tips: Influence Without Noise

GD is about constructive collaboration, not verbal wrestling.

You're being observed for leadership presence, listening skills, decision-making, and teamwork.

1. Enter the Discussion Early—But Not First Without Thought

Make your entry in the first 30–45 seconds.

If you have a solid point, go ahead. If not, listen first, then enter with clarity.

"Don't speak first to impress. Speak right to express."

2. Speak 2–3 Times, Not Continuously

Quality matters more than quantity.

Speak 2–3 times with relevance and impact. Don't try to dominate.

3. Build on Others' Ideas

Phrases like:

- "I agree with the point made by chest number 5, and I'd like to add…"

- "That's a good point. We could also include…"

- Show maturity and group spirit—a key OLQ.

4. Be the Peacemaker in Chaos

If the group becomes noisy or argumentative:

- Suggest a summary

- Redirect the discussion

- Calmly call for order

Assessors love candidates who bring calm to chaos.

5. Stay Composed—Even If You Get Interrupted

Never lose your cool. Wait, then speak again.

Your ability to stay grounded when ignored or challenged shows emotional balance—a leadership quality.

What to Avoid in Narration & GD

- Shouting or interrupting

- Speaking just for the sake of it

- Criticizing someone's story harshly

- Sitting casually or fidgeting

- Using overcomplicated words or fake accent

Practice Prompts:

Try narrating on these sample PPDT themes:

- A man looking at a railway track

- Three people standing near a car with a flat tyre

- A student sitting alone in a library

- A group of villagers outside a health camp

Then practice group discussion with friends using:

- "Let's agree on one central character and build around that."

- "Can we combine the two strongest points from these ideas?"

"In narration and GD, you're not trying to be the loudest.

You're trying to be the most clear, calm, and constructive voice in the room."

Be firm, not forceful.

Be humble, not hesitant.

Be the one who lifts the group—not the one who competes for the mic.

That's what officer material looks like.

Chapter 8

8. Day 2: Psychology Tests

Unveiling Your True Self—One Thought at a Time

Day 2 at the SSB is a deep dive into your mind.

No GTO tasks, no group dynamics—just you, your thoughts, and the psychologist.

This day is designed not to "test" you in the academic sense but to reveal your true personality—your instincts, mindset, values, and emotional framework.

Here, you don't need to impress.

You need to express—clearly, honestly, and naturally.

What Are Psychology Tests All About?

They help assessors understand:

- How you think under pressure

- How you make decisions

- What values drive you

- How emotionally balanced and socially effective you are

- Whether your Officer-Like Qualities (OLQs) are naturally present

These tests go beyond what you say in interviews—they tap into your inner wiring.

The Four Psychology Tests

1. Thematic Apperception Test (TAT)

"What's your worldview? How do you respond to life situations?"

- 12 slides (11 images + 1 blank)

- For each: 30 seconds to view, 4 minutes to write a story

- Use the format:

  o What led to the situation

  o What's happening now

  o What will be the outcome

Tips:

- Keep your stories realistic and socially meaningful

- Main character should show problem-solving, responsibility, and initiative

- Avoid fantasy, violence, or glorified endings

- Use the blank slide to tell a real story from your own life (leadership moment, challenge faced, etc.)

2. Word Association Test (WAT)

"What do you think in the first 5 seconds?"

- 60 words, one every 15 seconds

- You must write the first sentence that comes to mind

Tips:

- Keep sentences short, active, and positive

- Reflect clarity, confidence, and purpose

- Avoid negative words, fear-based responses, or memorized lines

- Focus on values like courage, truth, respect, service, discipline

3. Situation Reaction Test (SRT)

"How do you behave in real-world scenarios?"

- 60 situations in 30 minutes

- Respond with what you would do, not what's ideal

Tips:

- Think practically—show presence of mind, not perfection
- Responses should reflect responsibility, calmness, courage, and clarity
- Avoid extreme actions (violence, quitting, running away)
- Be time-efficient—short, decisive sentences

4. Self-Description Test (SDT)

"How well do you know yourself?"

- Write how you are perceived by:
    1. Parents
    2. Teachers/employers
    3. Friends
    4. Yourself
    5. What you want to improve

Tips:

- Be honest, balanced, and humble
- Include strengths and areas for growth

- Don't copy textbook phrases—be authentic

- Show self-awareness and a mindset for improvement

General Tips for Day 2:

Be Consistent Across All Tests

Your thinking pattern in TAT, WAT, and SRT should reflect a similar value system and maturity.

Stay Calm, Stay Present

Don't overthink or try to be ideal. Let your responses flow naturally.

Handwriting Matters—To a Point

Keep your writing legible and structured. Don't worry about beauty—focus on readability and clarity.

Time Management Is Crucial

You may not finish all SRTs—and that's okay. Quality > quantity. But with practice, aim to write 45–55 confidently.

What the Psychologist Is Looking For:

Quality	How It Appears
Clarity of Thought	Logical stories, direct responses, consistent tone
Responsibility	Owning outcomes, helping others, being accountable
Initiative	Characters taking action, SRT solutions with leadership
Emotional Maturity	Balanced reactions, no panic or extreme emotion
Authenticity	Natural self-description and realistic decision-making

What to Avoid:

- Writing memorized stories or model responses

- Using negative or fearful phrases

- Faking achievements or personality traits

- Writing what you *think* the board wants to hear

"Psychology Day is not about what you know.

It's about who you are—when you're not trying to perform."

So drop the fear. Drop the filters.

Let your truth come out—with awareness, confidence, and a sense of service.

That's how you pass not just the test—but the mirror.

8.1. Thematic Apperception Test (TAT)

Your Storytelling Speaks Louder Than You Think

The Thematic Apperception Test (TAT) is the first and most crucial test in the SSB Psychology series.

It doesn't judge your writing skills—it reveals your thinking patterns, emotional maturity, and leadership qualities through the stories you tell.

It's not about fiction. It's about reflection.

Not about performance—but personality.

What is the TAT?

- You will be shown 11 pictures (one at a time), followed by 1 blank slide

- For each image, you'll get:

o   30 seconds to observe the picture

o   4 minutes to write a story based on it

The psychologist wants to know:

"What does your mind see, and how do you process it under pressure?"

Structure of a Good TAT Story

Use this simple 3-step model for each story:

1. What led to the situation?

- Brief context about the setting or problem

2. What is happening now?

- Central action being taken by the main character (should reflect *you*)

- Show initiative, clarity, courage, or leadership

3. What will be the outcome?

- A positive, realistic, socially relevant result

- Avoid fantasy or over-idealism

Your Character = You

The main character in every story should reflect:

- Your age, background, and values

- Officer-like qualities: responsibility, empathy, decision-making, service mindset

- A realistic personality with clarity and growth potential

"Don't create a superhero. Create a sincere human being who responds with maturity and purpose."

What Makes a Strong TAT Story?

- Clear structure (beginning → middle → end)

- Logical, practical, and socially meaningful action

- Character-driven—not event-driven

- Realistic optimism (not fantasy or magic)

- Reflection of OLQs: initiative, empathy, responsibility, confidence

What to Avoid in TAT

- Heroic exaggeration (one person saving the world)

- Violence, revenge, or negativity

- Copy-paste stories from books or coaching

- Complex vocabulary—simple is powerful

- Incomplete endings or unclear conclusions

TAT Blank Slide – Your Moment of Truth

The 12th slide will be blank. You'll be asked to write a story without any visual clue.

This is your chance to:

- Share a real-life experience that shaped you

- Highlight a personal leadership moment

- Describe a difficult situation you overcame

"This slide is your mirror—use it to show the officer within."

Examples of TAT Themes You Might See:

Image	Possible Themes
A man staring at a building	Job loss, starting a business, helping his community
Students looking at a map	Planning a trip, organizing relief work, education awareness
A family in a room	Resolving a conflict, career decision, supporting parents

A person walking alone in rain	Inner struggle, self-reflection, physical endurance
The blank slide	Real personal story (campus project, sports leadership, helping someone in need, etc.)

Practice Prompts:

1. A group of people near a broken bridge

2. A girl reading a book alone in a library

3. Two men looking at a machine

4. A child standing with a policeman

5. Blank slide: Share a personal moment that shaped your values

"In TAT, you don't just write stories.

You reveal who you are when life puts you in the lead."

So breathe. Observe. Reflect.

And write from a place of clarity, responsibility, and quiet strength.

Because the pen is not just in your hand.

It's in your heart.

8.2. Word Association Test (WAT)

Where Every Word Reveals Your Worldview

The Word Association Test (WAT) is the second psychology test on Day 2 of the SSB.

It looks simple—but it's one of the most powerful tools used by the psychologist to understand your subconscious mind, thought process, attitude, and personality traits.

In WAT, the words speak to you.

But what you write in response? That speaks for you.

What Is the WAT?

- You'll be shown 60 words, one at a time

- Each word appears on the screen for 15 seconds only

- You must write a sentence immediately that reflects your first thought in response to the word

The idea?

"How do you react to life—under pressure, without filters?"

Objective of WAT

The psychologist uses WAT to assess:

- Your instinctive response patterns

- Your emotional stability

- Your worldview and values

- Whether you reflect Officer-Like Qualities (OLQs) naturally in your thinking

You can't fake WAT—your patterns will show.

How to Respond to WAT Words

The key is clarity, positivity, and practicality.

Here's a sample flow:

Word	Weak Response	Strong Response
Fail	I hate failure	Failure teaches lessons
Discipline	Discipline is hard	Discipline builds character
War	War is dangerous	Army prevents war through strength
Friend	Friend betrayed me	Friend supports in tough times
Risk	Risk is scary	Smart risks lead to growth

Tips for Writing WAT Sentences

1. Use Active, Positive Sentences

- Show leadership, optimism, responsibility

- Avoid negative phrasing like "never," "hate," "can't," "failure is bad"

- Even serious topics (death, fear, defeat) can be responded to with maturity

2. Be Natural, Not Theatrical

- Don't force big words or sound like a philosopher

- Keep your tone genuine and relatable

3. Let Your OLQs Shine Through

- Values like courage, empathy, teamwork, initiative, and service should appear organically in your responses

4. Write Quickly, Don't Overthink

- Trust your preparation

- Let your real mindset respond—not a rehearsed one

"15 seconds is not time to perform. It's time to reflect who you truly are."

How WAT Connects with Other Tests

Assessors will cross-reference your WAT responses with:

- Your TAT stories

- Your SRT reactions

- Your Self-Description

Consistency in values, tone, and mindset = genuine personality

Inconsistency or contradictions = red flags

WAT Practice Examples

Try writing one-line responses to the following:

1. Success

2. Team

3. Pain

4. Leader

5. Change

6. Alone

7. Honesty

8. Goal

9. Danger

10. Peace

Practice writing within 15 seconds each to simulate test conditions.

Common Mistakes to Avoid

- Writing memorized sentences from books or coaching notes

- Using negative language repeatedly

- Giving unrelated or vague responses

- Being too philosophical or artificial

- Repeating the same kind of sentence pattern for every word

"In WAT, your response is not a line. It's a window—to your thoughts, values, and emotional strength."

So prepare not just with your pen, but with your perspective.

Think clearly. Write naturally.

And let your words reflect the kind of leader the forces are proud to train.

8.3. Situation Reaction Test (SRT)

Where Your Real Personality Takes the Lead

The Situation Reaction Test (SRT) is the third psychological test in the SSB.

Here, you're not just answering questions—you're revealing how your mind works in action.

In real life, officers must think fast, act decisively, and remain balanced in all situations.

That's exactly what the SRT checks:

"How do you think and act when life throws you a challenge?"

What Is the SRT?

- You'll be given 60 real-life situations

- You'll have 30 minutes to respond

- You must write your reactions—not long essays, just short, practical, clear actions

It's a test of your decision-making, emotional balance, responsibility, courage, and maturity.

What Does the Psychologist Look For?

They want to see:

- Presence of mind

- Clarity under pressure

- Responsibility without excuses

- Confidence without arrogance

- Leadership without show-off

More than what you write, they assess how you think and whether you have Officer-Like Qualities (OLQs) in your decisions.

How to Frame SRT Responses

Use the 3Cs formula:

Clear

Confident

Constructive

Example Situations:

Situation	Weak Reaction	Strong Reaction
You are late for your duty.	I panic and rush.	Informs senior, takes fastest route, apologizes, ensures it won't repeat.
Your friend fails in exams and is depressed.	I tell him to forget it.	Motivates him, suggests steps for improvement, stays in touch for support.
You are alone and see a road accident.	I feel scared.	Takes victim to hospital, informs police and family.
You are short of money while traveling.	I cancel the trip.	Informs parents, arranges alternate help, continues journey.
Your team is not cooperating.	I work alone.	Talks to team, explains goal, motivates them to work together.

Tips to Ace the SRT

1. Be Action-Oriented

- Show what you would do, not what you think or feel

- Write decisive actions, not vague ideas

2. Be Realistic, Not Filmy

- Don't try to be a superhero

- Think like a responsible, emotionally balanced person

3. Be Practical & Prioritize Safety

- React logically under emergencies

- Think of people's well-being

- Show presence of mind

4. Stay Positive and Proactive

- Your responses should reflect optimism, not fear or helplessness

- Take initiative, don't wait for others to solve the problem

5. Manage Time Well

- Aim to complete at least 45–55 situations

- Don't get stuck—keep your responses brief and clear

Common Mistakes to Avoid

- Writing long, unclear answers

- Giving emotional or impractical reactions

- Ignoring key responsibilities (e.g., not informing anyone during emergencies)

- Avoiding tough situations or showing indecisiveness

- Using passive responses like "He should..." instead of "I will..."

Practice Prompts

Try responding to these quickly in your notebook:

1. You lost your important documents a day before your interview.

2. Your leader takes a wrong decision in a team task.

3. You're the only one in your group who completes a task early.

4. You see a fire break out in the hostel.

5. You disagree with your friend's opinion in public.

"In the SRT, you don't write what sounds ideal.

You write what shows you're ready to lead under pressure."

So train your thinking to be sharp, responsible, and clear.

And when the situation demands a reaction—respond with strength, not confusion.

That's the mindset that earns stars on the shoulder.

8.4.Self-Description Test (SDT)

The Mirror You Hold Up to Your Mind

The Self-Description Test (SDT) is the final psychological test in the SSB.

It's not a test of grammar or style—it's a test of self-awareness.

It asks you a simple question that many struggle to answer:

"Who are you—really?"

You're not judged on perfection. You're judged on how well you know yourself, how honestly you can reflect, and how open you are to growth.

What Is the SDT?

You will be asked to write how you are perceived by:

1. Your Parents

2. Your Teachers or Employers

3. Your Friends

4. Yourself

5. What You Would Like to Improve in Yourself

You'll get 15–20 minutes to complete this, often on the same answer sheet as the other psychology tests.

Purpose of the SDT

The psychologist is looking for:

- Honesty – Are you truthful about your flaws and strengths?

- Balance – Do you acknowledge both praise and criticism?

- Maturity – Can you reflect without blame or exaggeration?

- Growth mindset – Are you willing to evolve?

This test connects with your entire personality shown in the TAT, WAT, SRT, and interview. If your SDT is authentic, it adds depth and credibility to everything else.

How to Write Each Section

1. Parents' Opinion

Reflect how your family sees you at home—your habits, values, responsibilities.

Example:

"My parents see me as a responsible and caring individual. They appreciate my discipline, honesty, and dedication to studies. At times, they advise me to be more relaxed and enjoy life outside academics."

2. Teachers/Employers' Opinion

This reflects your behavior in a formal setting—your attitude, discipline, and team orientation.

Example:

"My teachers consider me a sincere and attentive student who actively participates in class and takes responsibility in group projects. They suggest I speak up more confidently during public discussions."

3. Friends' Opinion

What are you like in a peer group? Friendly? Trustworthy? Supportive?

Example:

"My friends see me as a reliable and supportive companion. They often seek my help in personal and academic matters. Some of them wish I would socialize more actively during group events."

4. Your Own View

This is your core self-awareness. Be honest, humble, and balanced.

Example:

"I see myself as a curious and sincere person who enjoys learning and helping others. I stay calm in pressure situations and take initiative in solving problems. I feel I can still improve my assertiveness and communication skills."

5. Areas of Improvement

This shows emotional maturity and a growth mindset. Avoid generic answers like "I want to be perfect."

Example:

"I am working on improving my public speaking skills and expressing my thoughts more confidently in group settings. I also want to manage my time better by reducing distractions."

Tips for a Powerful SDT

- Keep it real. Avoid textbook-style lines or over-polished praise.

- Be brief but specific. Around 4–5 lines per section is enough.

- Show balance. Combine strengths with small, practical areas of improvement.

- Use simple language. It's not a writing contest—it's a reflection exercise.

- Practice—but don't memorize. Stay consistent with your personality.

Mistakes to Avoid

- Copying generic answers like: "Everyone loves me."

- Hiding all weaknesses or writing none

- Being overly negative or critical of yourself

- Using fake or exaggerated qualities

- Writing in third person (always write in first person)

"SDT is where you stop trying to 'clear' the test—and simply choose to connect with yourself."

It's your chance to show that you're:

- Aware of your gifts

- Grateful for your influences

- Humble about your growth areas

- Ready to evolve as a future officer

Because leadership begins with self-leadership.

Chapter 9

9. Day 3 & 4: Group Tasks with the GTO

Where You Don't Just Talk Like a Leader—You Act Like One

Welcome to one of the most dynamic and revealing phases of your SSB journey: the Group Testing Officer (GTO) tasks.

Conducted over Day 3 and 4, these tasks take you beyond theory, beyond psychology—and place you directly into team-based action.

This is where your true colors as a leader, team player, decision-maker, and problem-solver come out—not just in what you say, but in how you behave, perform, and contribute.

Who Is the GTO?

The Group Testing Officer observes you through a series of outdoor and indoor tasks.

He doesn't speak much—but he sees everything:

- Your initiative

- Your cooperation

- Your stamina

- Your presence of mind

- Your body language and team spirit

And most importantly—your natural Officer-Like Qualities (OLQs).

List of GTO Tasks

Task No.	Name	Type
1	Group Discussion (GD)	Indoor (Verbal)
2	Group Planning Exercise (GPE)	Indoor (Analytical/Verbal)
3	Progressive Group Task (PGT)	Outdoor (Physical + Strategy)
4	Group Obstacle Race (GOR)	Outdoor (Fun + Team Spirit)
5	Half Group Task (HGT)	Outdoor (Focused Leadership)

6	Lecturette	Individual (Public Speaking)
7	Individual Obstacles (IO)	Physical (Stamina + Grit)
8	Command Task (CT)	Outdoor (Leadership & Thinking)
9	Final Group Task (FGT)	Outdoor (Group Wrap-up)

Let's dive into each of them.

1. Group Discussion (GD)

Two rounds. One with a factual topic, the second with a more abstract or social issue.

Tips:

- Be an early but meaningful speaker

- Show listening skills

- Build on others' ideas

- Avoid shouting or dominating

- Be clear, relevant, and respectful

"Don't aim to impress. Aim to progress the discussion."

2. Group Planning Exercise (GPE)

A situation-based problem is given (usually involving emergencies, maps, and timelines). You must:

- Read the story

- Understand the issues

- Write an individual solution

- Discuss and agree on a common group plan

- One candidate presents the final plan

Tips:

- Be logical, practical, and time-sensitive

- Divide responsibilities and use resources wisely

- Be the one who connects ideas and resolves confusion

3. Progressive Group Task (PGT)

Outdoor task involving a series of physical obstacles to cross as a team using helping material (planks, ropes, etc.).

Tips:

- Understand the rules (Rule of color, distance, rigidity)

- Speak up with ideas, but allow others too

- Be energetic and helpful—not controlling

- Never just stand around—stay involved

"Your hands should be working. Your mind should be thinking. Your energy should be lifting the group."

4. Group Obstacle Race (GOR)

A fun, competitive "snake race" where groups race while carrying a load (a rolled-up snake-like object), crossing multiple obstacles together.

Tips:

- Shout slogans together—boost morale

- Be physically active and encouraging

- Don't drag the team—push it forward

- Help those who struggle—real teamwork is tested here

5. Half Group Task (HGT)

Similar to PGT, but with half the group. You get more visibility, so use it well.

Tips:

- Speak with more clarity

- Guide and support teammates

- Show leadership and humility together

- Give smart solutions—be clear and assertive, not bossy

6. Lecturette

You pick 1 topic out of 4 and speak for 3 minutes in front of the group.

Tips:

- Use a 3-part structure: Intro, Body, Conclusion

- Speak with confidence, not speed

- Make eye contact with all

- Stay composed even if you forget—bounce back naturally

- Pick a topic you know well

7. Individual Obstacles (IO)

10 obstacles in 3 minutes. Each has a score from 1 to 10. You can repeat once done.

Tips:

- Plan ahead: do easier ones first

- Stay focused—not fearful

- Don't give up if you fall—resilience is key

- Show fitness, willpower, and strategy

8. Command Task (CT)

You are made a leader. Choose 2 subordinates and lead them across an obstacle using limited materials.

Tips:

- Give clear instructions

- Be respectful but firm with subordinates

- Show smart decision-making

- When the GTO chats with you—stay calm, be honest

9. Final Group Task (FGT)

Last outdoor group task—like PGT, but usually shorter and symbolic.

Tips:

- Don't become silent or over-relaxed

- Stay involved

- Reinforce team spirit—close strong

What the GTO Looks For

Trait	How It Shows
Leadership	Voluntary involvement, initiative, calm authority
Cooperation	Supporting teammates, encouraging quieter members
Practical Intelligence	Smart planning in tasks like GPE and CT
Courage	Facing obstacles confidently
Communication	Clear speech in Lecturette, GD, CT
Team Spirit	Celebrating together, staying composed in chaos

"You don't have to be the best at everything.

You just have to be the kind of person everyone trusts, listens to, and wants to follow."

So show up with energy, clarity, humility, and heart.

Let the team succeed—and let your presence make the team better.

That's what officer material is made of.

Group Discussions & Planning Exercises

Where Thinking, Speaking, and Leading Come Together

On Day 3 of the SSB, the first impression you make on your Group Testing Officer (GTO) happens not with your body—but with your mind and mouth.

The Group Discussion (GD) and Group Planning Exercise (GPE) are indoor tasks where your mental sharpness, clarity, communication, and group behavior are on full display.

In these tasks, the assessors are silently asking:

"Can this candidate think logically, speak clearly, and lead respectfully in a team setting?"

Let's explore each task in depth.

9.1. Group Discussion (GD)

You'll have two rounds of GD:

1. A current affairs or factual topic

2. A social or abstract topic (e.g., "Success is a journey," "Technology is a double-edged sword")

There is no moderator—it's a free-flowing, self-managed discussion among 8–10 candidates.

Objective of GD

- To test your clarity of thought, communication style, and team spirit

- To observe how you express yourself under pressure

- To assess your listening and influencing skills

Tips for a Strong GD Performance

1. Start Early (But Not Blindly)

Try to speak in the first 30–60 seconds. If you have a valid point, make it.

A good start shows initiative—but don't force it if you're unsure.

2. Be Relevant, Not Repetitive

Speak 2–3 times with meaningful input, rather than speaking just for volume.

3. Support Others' Ideas

Build on good points made by others. This shows maturity and teamwork.

4. Calm the Chaos

If the group gets noisy, try to bring order with lines like:

"Let's give everyone a chance,"

"We all seem to agree on this point—shall we move forward?"

5. Watch Your Body Language

- Sit straight

- Maintain gentle eye contact

- Avoid pointing fingers or crossing arms

- Smile when appropriate—composure is leadership

"In GD, you are not just sharing ideas. You are shaping group energy."

9.2. Group Planning Exercise (GPE)

Also called Military Planning Exercise, this is a scenario-based group task that simulates real-world emergencies or challenges.

You'll receive a:

- Situation-based story (with 4–5 problems)

- Map with distances, timelines, and resources

- Instructions to write your individual plan first, then discuss and present a group plan

Structure of a GPE Solution

1. Identify and list problems clearly

2. Prioritize based on urgency and impact

3. Allocate resources and divide team roles

4. Stick to the timeline

5. Provide a clear conclusion

Tips for GPE Success

1. Stay Calm While Reading

- Underline key details

- Note the time, distance, team size, and transport options

2. Be Logical, Not Heroic

- Don't try to solve all problems personally

- Distribute tasks wisely—delegation is leadership

3. Use Time Efficiently

- Don't waste time debating too much in the group phase

- Contribute clearly and constructively

4. Show Flexibility

- If someone has a better idea, support it

- Maturity is knowing when to lead and when to adapt

5. Summarize with Confidence

If you're chosen to present the final plan, be clear, concise, and composed.

Even if not chosen, support the speaker.

What the GTO Observes in GD & GPE

Trait	Indicator
Initiative	Speaking first with a strong point
Clarity	Well-structured arguments
Logic	Prioritizing actions in GPE with valid reasoning
Cooperation	Listening, including others, staying calm
Leadership	Guiding group decisions without dominating

Common Mistakes to Avoid

- Interrupting or arguing aggressively

- Memorized content with no real understanding

- Over-assertiveness or passivity

- Ignoring others' input

- Fixating on one solution without flexibility

"In GD and GPE, your goal is not to show you're better—it's to show that you make the group better."

Speak with calm confidence.

Think like a problem-solver.

Act like the leader who listens before leading.

That's how officer material stands out—silently, strongly, and with clarity.

9.3. Progressive Group Task (PGT)

Where Strategy Meets Strength—and the Team Meets the Real You

The Progressive Group Task (PGT) is often one of the most exciting and revealing outdoor activities in the SSB process.

It's where the board wants to see not just how smart you are, but how you apply that smartness on the ground, with people, under constraints.

The task is not about who finishes first.

It's about who steps up, works together, and thinks like an officer under open skies.

What Is the PGT?

In the PGT, your group (usually 8–10 candidates) must cross a series of obstacle structures, using only:

- A plank

- A rope

- A load-carrying object (like a drum or box)

You must move from a start line to an end line, crossing obstacles (represented by marked ground, planks, platforms, etc.)—without touching the ground or violating the rules.

Each level becomes progressively more difficult—hence, *Progressive Group Task*.

What It Tests

- Teamwork

- Initiative and leadership

- Practical intelligence

- Communication under pressure

- Adaptability and patience

- Awareness of rules and planning

The GTO observes you from a distance—he doesn't interfere or guide you.

"This is not a test of fitness alone—it's a test of functionality in a group under constraint."

Golden Rules of GTO Tasks (Apply to PGT Too)

These rules are strictly enforced, and breaking them can affect your recommendation.

Rule	Meaning
Rule of Distance	You cannot jump a distance greater than 4 feet
Rule of Color	Only white surfaces are usable; red means out-of-bounds
Rule of Rigidity	You can only tie/plank/connect with rigid surfaces—no flexible structures like ropes

Rule of Load	Carry the load throughout—it is symbolic of teamwork/responsibility
Rule of Group	Always work together—never rush ahead or leave others behind

Tips to Perform Well in PGT

1. Understand the Rules Before You Begin

Ask the GTO if you are unsure about a rule. Once the task starts, you won't get clarifications.

2. Think Aloud—Communicate Clearly

Share your ideas out loud, even if they're not perfect.

Speaking up shows initiative and analytical thinking.

3. Be a Doer, Not a Dictator

- Suggest plans

- Place planks

- Support others

- Be hands-on and involved

"A real leader lifts the team—physically and mentally."

4. Stay Involved, Even Without the Plank

If others are using the materials, don't stand idle. Encourage, stabilize structures, manage the load, or help guide the action.

5. Respect All Contributions

Don't dismiss others' ideas. Build on them.

Include quieter group members—they may have good insights.

6. Stay Calm in Confusion

When the group gets stuck or argues, step in with solutions or suggest a pause to replan.

This shows composure and command under pressure.

What the GTO Observes in PGT

Quality	How It Appears
Leadership	Giving ideas, taking initiative, motivating others
Cooperation	Helping, listening, team-first behavior
Practical Thinking	Smart use of resources, applying the rules
Communication	Speaking clearly and respectfully

Determination	Staying active and engaged till the end

Common Mistakes to Avoid

- Standing idle or silent

- Shouting or dominating the team

- Ignoring safety or rule violations

- Getting frustrated or giving up

- Clinging to your own idea even when it's not working

"In PGT, you don't have to be the hero.

You just have to be the one who holds the team together, step by step."

So walk into it with:

- A clear head

- A collaborative heart

- And a courageous mindset

Because when the GTO sees someone who can think, lead, and adapt in motion—he sees officer material.

9.4. Group Obstacle Race (GOR)

The Snake Race That Reveals Your Spirit

Also known as the "Snake Race", the Group Obstacle Race (GOR) is one of the most energetic, exciting, and revealing tasks in the GTO series.

This task is not about individual brilliance. It's about team energy, cooperation, adaptability, and motivation.

And while the GTO may laugh along with your group during the fun, he's carefully observing how you behave under pressure, confusion, and physical challenge.

"It's not who crosses first. It's how you take everyone with you."

What is the GOR?

- Your group is given a heavy rolled-up object (the "snake"), which must be carried throughout the race.

- You must cross 6–10 obstacles as a team.

- Everyone—including the snake—must pass through each obstacle.

- Rules apply for safety and fairness, and any violation may cause penalties (restart, time delay, etc.).

Objectives of GOR

- Test your team spirit and group coordination

- Observe your physical involvement and enthusiasm

- See how you handle chaotic situations

- Identify your supportiveness, resilience, and motivation skills

Common Obstacles You May Face

1. Zig-zag beams

2. Wall climb

3. Rope crawl

4. Spider's web (pass through gaps)

5. Slippery ramp

6. Tunnel crawl

7. Balance beams

8. Net jump or net climb

Each obstacle requires smart planning, equal effort, and safe teamwork.

Tips to Excel in GOR

1. Be the Team Engine

- Volunteer to carry the snake—it's not easy, but shows leadership

- If you're not holding it, support others who are by guiding or stabilizing

2. Follow the Rules Seriously

- Do not jump too far, skip steps, or ignore the snake

- The whole team + the snake must cross each obstacle

- Keep the snake off the ground unless permitted

3. Motivate Others Loudly and Positively

- Cheer for your team:

"Let's go, together!"

"We've got this—next one!"

- Use slogans or chants if your group enjoys that energy (it's encouraged)

"An officer doesn't just do. He helps others do better."

4. Be Alert and Physically Active

- Assist team members climbing or landing

- Stay focused—tiredness is no excuse to zone out

- Be safe, but energetic and fully involved

5. Avoid Confusion and Conflicts

- Don't argue in the middle of the task

- If someone falls behind or struggles, help them instead of blaming

What the GTO Observes During GOR

Trait	How It Shows
Team Spirit	Equal participation, unity, motivation
Cooperation	Supporting the slow or struggling members
Stamina	Sustained effort through all obstacles
Leadership	Volunteering, organizing, encouraging
Adaptability	Responding positively to chaos or delays

Mistakes to Avoid

- Refusing to hold or help with the snake

- Losing temper or blaming teammates

- Trying to show off individually

- Disobeying rules (jumping beyond limits, skipping turns)

- Mentally quitting halfway through

"The GOR is not a race of legs—it's a race of hearts working in sync."

So be the one who:

- Holds the team up when it slows down

- Smiles when others struggle

- Shouts encouragement when things fall apart

- Finishes strong—not alone, but together

Because that's the kind of leader the GTO will never forget.

9.5. Half Group Task (HGT)

Your Focused Window of Leadership

In HGT, your group is split into two halves (usually 4–5 candidates). You'll face a single obstacle, similar to the PGT format, and solve it together with materials like planks, ropes, and load.

Smaller group = more visibility for each candidate.

This is often the GTO's "confirmation test"—he watches more closely to see if what you showed earlier was genuine.

Tips for HGT Success

1. Take the Lead—but Don't Dominate

You now have space to show leadership clearly. Use it by:

- Giving clear, actionable suggestions

- Helping arrange materials

- Moving with purpose

- Listening actively

2. Stay Respectful

The group is smaller, so your attitude stands out even more. Be encouraging, not bossy.

3. Be Hands-On

Don't just talk—act. Fix planks, lift loads, offer physical help.

4. Stay Consistent

The GTO compares this to your PGT behavior. Don't suddenly become aggressive or go completely silent.

What the GTO Is Watching in HGT

- Are you consistent with your earlier performance?

- Do you share space, or try to steal the spotlight?

- Are you a team enabler, not just a task solver?

- Can you stay calm, thoughtful, and practical when the group is watching you closely?

9.6. Lecturette: Speaking with Impact

Because One Clear Voice Can Reflect a Strong Mind

The Lecturette is your personal stage—your opportunity to show how well you think, how clearly you speak, and how confidently you carry yourself.

It's not about being a flawless orator. It's about being a thoughtful communicator.

In just 3 minutes, the GTO wants to see if you can:

"Organize your thoughts, express them with conviction, and carry your presence with calm strength."

What Is the Lecturette?

- Each candidate gets a set of 4 topics on a card

- You choose one topic

- You get 3 minutes to prepare

- Then, you stand in front of the group and speak for 3 minutes

No interruptions. No questions. Just you, your voice, and your message.

Purpose of the Lecturette

The GTO is looking at:

- Clarity of thought

- Confidence and composure

- Body language and delivery

- Logical structuring of content

- Awareness and presence of mind

"This is not a public speaking contest. It's a test of leadership presence under silent observation."

Tips for Choosing the Right Topic

- Pick the one you know most about, not the one that *sounds best*

- Avoid choosing something just because others think it's "tough" or "impressive"

- Confidence > Content. Choose what you can explain well.

3-Minute Structure for Lecturette (Simple & Powerful)

1. Introduction (30 sec)

- Define the topic

- State why it matters (local/national/global relevance)

2. Body (1.5–2 min)

- Give 2–3 main points or arguments

- Use simple logic, relevant facts, or examples

- Stay focused and connected to the topic

3. Conclusion (30 sec)

- Summarize your key message

- End with a strong line: insight, solution, or quote

Tips to Speak with Impact

1. Stand Tall, Breathe Easy

Posture = presence. Stand naturally, look around the group, and take a deep breath before you begin.

2. Speak Clearly—Not Fast

Your goal is clarity, not speed. Let every word land.

3. Use a Confident but Natural Tone

No need for a fake accent or dramatic delivery. Be authentic, steady, and engaged.

4. Use Simple Language

Big words don't build big impact—clear thoughts do.

5. Maintain Eye Contact

Don't stare at one person. Sweep across the group gently, showing confidence.

Sample Topics You Might Get

General Topics	Social/Abstract Topics	Current Affairs
Role of youth in nation-building	Money vs Happiness	India's G20 presidency

Social media: boon or bane?	Discipline in life	Artificial Intelligence
Environment conservation	Success and failure	Women in the Armed Forces
Importance of education	Time management	India's Defence Budget

Practice Drill (3-3-3 Rule)

- 3 minutes to prepare

- 3 minutes to speak

- 3 topics per day for 3 days

This builds comfort, structure, and fluency before the real task.

Common Mistakes to Avoid

- Freezing due to overthinking

- Over-reliance on memorized content

- Repeating points or going off-topic

- Using slang, jokes, or filler words (umm, like, you know)

- Apologizing or showing nervousness

"Your voice is your leadership in action."

The Lecturette shows whether you can:

- Stand tall in front of others

- Think clearly under time pressure

- And speak not to impress—but to influence with clarity

So, don't aim to deliver a perfect speech.

Aim to speak with conviction, connection, and calmness.

That's what makes you officer material.

9.7. Individual Obstacles (IO)

Where Your Body Follows Your Mind, and Your Spirit Leads Both.

In the journey to becoming an officer, there are moments when teamwork matters, and others when it's just you and the task in front of you.

The Individual Obstacles (IO) test is one such moment. No support, no group—just you, your courage, and your composure.

This task is not just a test of your physical ability. It's a mirror of your mental resilience, planning under pressure, and attitude toward risk and failure.

Purpose of the IO Test

The GTO wants to assess:

Your physical stamina and coordination

Fear-handling ability (heights, jumps, balance, etc.)

Mental agility under time pressure

Attitude when faced with failure (Do you give up or go again?)

Consistency in showing initiative, determination, and spirit

"It's not about how fast you are. It's about how you face difficulty—alone, and without excuses."

Structure and Scoring

Number of Obstacles: Usually 10

Time Allotted: 3 minutes

Scoring: Each obstacle has a number painted on it (1–10)—that's its score

Repeat Option: If you finish all 10 before time, you can repeat obstacles to increase your score

Max Possible Score: 55–60 (with repetition)

Common Obstacles:

Double Ditch Jump

Zig-Zag Balance Beam

Rope Climb

Wall Jump

Monkey Crawl on Horizontal Rope

Long Jump

Tyre Jump

Tarzan Swing

Double Platform Leap

Belly Crawl Under Bars

Some are about speed. Others test balance or upper-body strength. All test mental sharpness under physical effort.

Tips to Perform with Clarity and Character

Before the Task

Observe each obstacle during the demo carefully

Mentally map your sequence—go from easy to hard, or in a pattern that fits your strengths

Do light stretching and warm-up—avoid injury

During the Task

Start fast but controlled—don't panic

Attempt each obstacle even if you fear failure (effort matters)

If you fall, recover quickly and move on—time is more valuable than ego

Prioritize high-score obstacles if you're confident in them

After the Task:

Do not complain, compare, or over-explain

Carry yourself with grace—even if you missed some

Your body language after the test also gets observed

What the GTO is Really Looking For

Quality	How It's Revealed
Courage	Trying difficult obstacles without hesitation
Endurance	Maintaining energy and speed throughout
Clarity	Choosing the right sequence based on ability

Consistency	No erratic behavior or over-dramatic reactions
Resilience	Not stopping after failure or slip
Attitude	Completing with a sense of ownership and composure

Mental Framing for Success

This is not a gym competition.

It's a test of how you push yourself, alone, under pressure—just like life in uniform.

Even if you're not the fittest in the batch, your determination, presence of mind, and effort can leave a lasting impression.

Remember

"Anyone can look strong in a photo. But an officer is made in moments where strength is needed the most—when you are alone, tired, and out of breath, yet still moving forward."

9.8. Command Task (CT)

Where Leadership is Seen, Not Claimed.

In the journey of becoming an officer, the Command Task is the moment where the spotlight subtly shifts to you—not to show off, but to step up.

The GTO silently observes not just how you solve the problem, but how you handle people, pressure, and decision-making. It's less about building bridges, and more about building confidence in your ability to lead others with purpose and clarity.

Purpose of the Command Task

The Command Task tests:

Leadership under pressure

Decision-making and planning speed

Clarity of instruction and communication

Confidence and initiative

Handling of subordinates

Rule-following and flexibility

"This is not a task to prove dominance. It's a task to display direction with dignity."

Structure of the Task

GTO will call you individually, usually after HGT or before FGT.

He'll chat informally to put you at ease and then introduce the task setup.

You'll be shown an obstacle with helping materials (planks, ropes, etc.).

You must choose 2–3 subordinates (usually from your group).

You are the Commander: explain your plan, give orders, and execute.

Time: Usually 8–10 minutes to complete the task.

GTO may increase difficulty mid-task to test adaptability.

What the GTO Observes

Quality	How It's Revealed
Clarity	How well you visualize, plan, and explain your idea
Character	Confidence, control, and conduct under stress
Communication	Clear, firm, respectful instructions
Adaptability	Handling surprise or rule changes gracefully

| Responsibility | Ensuring everyone follows the rules and stays safe |
| Composure | Calm and firm even when things go wrong |

How to Approach the Command Task

Before You Start:

Study the obstacle carefully

Think through the solution before calling your subordinates

Choose subordinates wisely—those who listen and cooperate

While Executing:

Brief your team clearly and confidently

Give orders—not suggestions (but stay polite)

Physically involve yourself—lead by doing

Stick to rules; if broken, take remedial action immediately

Adapt fast if GTO modifies the setup mid-task

After the Task

Thank your subordinates

Share alternate solutions if GTO asks

Walk out with the same energy and respect you walked in with

Communication Tips

Speak firmly and clearly

Use names of subordinates to give direction

Don't ask: "Should we do this?" → Say: "Let's do this."

Avoid shouting or over-commanding

Stay engaged and encouraging without losing authority

Officer Qualities in Action

This task is not about being bossy or fast—it's about being:

Calm under stress

Quick to think, but slow to panic

Inclusive, yet firm

Solution-focused, not problem-focused

"The best commanders are followed not out of fear, but out of clarity and trust."

In the Words of a Veteran

"Command Task is a glimpse into how you'll lead men one day—not just with your mind, but with your presence. It's not about building a bridge with planks. It's about building confidence in others that they're safe when you're in charge."

Insight

Command Task is one of the most critical observations in GTO series.

You might forget your solution later, but the GTO will remember how you made decisions, how you treated your team, and how you carried yourself as a leader.

That's what being officer material is all about.

9.9. Final Group Task (FGT)

The Grand Finale—More Symbolic, Still Significant

Your Final Outdoor Opportunities to Be Seen—and Remembered

After the energy of the PGT ,GOR, and Half Group Task (HGT) , the Final Group Task (FGT) give you one more chances to show what kind of leader, teammate, and thinker you really are.

These tasks are often quieter, more focused—and just as critical.

Because by this point, the GTO has seen a lot. Now, he's looking for consistency, maturity, and calm leadership under pressure.

The FGT is the last GTO task. It's a group activity similar to the PGT, but usually:

- Shorter in length

- Less complex

- More about teamwork than task completion

This is a final chance for your group to bond, collaborate, and finish strong.

Tips for FGT Impact

1. Don't Switch Off

Many aspirants mentally "relax" in the FGT. Don't.

This may be the moment when the GTO makes his final note about your attitude and involvement.

2. Stay Positive and Team-Oriented

Be the one who helps others finish well.

If a teammate struggles—support them visibly.

3. Reflect Group Spirit

Your tone, teamwork, and involvement in this task send a strong message:

"Even at the end—I'm here for the team."

What Not to Do in HGT & FGT

- Going silent because "it's almost over"

- Suddenly trying to dominate in HGT

- Treating FGT like a formality

- Letting frustration or tiredness show

- Arguing with groupmates or pushing too hard

"These may be the final tasks—but they often leave the first impression in the GTO's final notes."

So approach HGT with quiet clarity.

And step into FGT with gratitude and group energy.

Let your presence reflect someone who doesn't just want to win a task—but wants to lift the team till the very last step.

That's the presence that stays with the board long after the task ends.

10. DAY 4: PERSONAL INTERVIEW PREPARATION

Speak Your Truth—Calmly, Clearly, and Confidently

Your personal interview is a vital part of the SSB process—often held on Day 2, 3, or 4, depending on scheduling.

If it's your turn on Day 4, this is your golden chance to sit face-to-face with the Interviewing Officer (IO) and share the story only you can tell: your own.

But this is no ordinary Q&A.

The IO isn't testing memory or mock answers.

He's searching for clarity, consistency, confidence, and character.

"In the interview, you don't need to impress.

You need to express—with authenticity and presence."

Interview Basics

- Duration: 30–60 minutes

- Setting: One-on-one, formal yet friendly

- Style: Conversational—but deeply analytical

- Focus: Your personality, mindset, decisions, awareness, and potential

The IO usually has your PIQ form (Personal Information Questionnaire) in front of him. Every question is likely to connect to it—so honesty and self-awareness are key.

Areas You'll Be Asked About

1. Personal Background

- Family, upbringing, values

- Strengths, habits, routine, hobbies

- Friends and how they see you

- Important life experiences

Be natural. Speak as you would to a respectful elder or mentor.

2. Education and Academics

- Subjects you like/dislike

- Performance and gaps, if any

- Projects or teamwork experiences

- Why you chose your stream or college

Avoid blaming teachers or circumstances. Focus on what you learned.

3. Work Experience (if applicable)

- Roles, responsibilities, what you enjoy

- Teamwork, deadlines, conflicts

- Why you want to switch to the armed forces

Be respectful of your current/previous role—even if you're leaving it.

4. Hobbies & Interests

- What do you do in your free time?

- Books, sports, games, music, creative arts

- Are you consistent with your interests?

Pick genuine hobbies. If you say "reading," be ready to name a book you actually read.

5. Current Affairs & General Awareness

- National & international issues

- Defence updates, government schemes

- Social challenges, environment, economy

Read a newspaper daily or follow a trusted news source.

6. Why the Armed Forces?

This is your purpose question.

Be clear, honest, and specific. Avoid clichés like "I love the uniform." Instead, say:

"I want a life of meaning, challenge, and contribution—aligned with my values and personality."

7. Situational & Psychological Questions

- What would you do if... (your plan fails, your teammate disagrees, etc.)

- How do you handle failure, stress, and criticism?

- What are your short- and long-term goals?

Stay calm. Reflect before answering. Honesty > idealism.

Tips to Prepare Effectively

1. Know Your PIQ Inward Out

- Review your personal, academic, and extracurricular details

- Be ready to explain every activity you've mentioned

- Cross-check for consistency across psych tests

2. Practice Self-Reflection

- Ask yourself: *"Why do I think/act this way?"*

- Journal your responses to mock interview questions

- Build emotional clarity

3. Mock Interviews with Honest Feedback

- Practice with a mentor, friend, or coach

- Record yourself to improve tone, posture, and flow

4. Stay Updated & Relevant

- Prepare key facts about the Indian Armed Forces

- Know about NDA/CDS/OTA (whichever you're applying for)

- Be aware of global events and current national developments

What the Interviewing Officer Observes

Quality	How It Shows
Clarity	Straightforward, structured answers
Confidence	Calm tone, eye contact, composure
Sincerity	Honest acceptance of gaps or weaknesses
Consistency	No contradiction with PIQ or psych tests
Decision-making	Logical, mature responses to situational questions
Motivation	Clear purpose behind choosing the Armed Forces

Common Mistakes to Avoid

- Memorizing answers

- Trying to sound over-idealistic

- Hiding failures or blaming others

- Giving general answers to specific questions

- Being too casual or too tense

"Your interview is not a challenge.

It's a conversation—a window into the mindset of a future officer."

So walk in with:

- Honesty in your heart

- Clarity in your mind

- Confidence in your tone

- And gratitude for the opportunity

Let the IO meet not the perfect you—but the prepared, purpose-driven, real you.

10.1. Crafting Your Story

Because You're Not Just a Candidate—You're a Journey

Every SSB aspirant walks into the selection center with something more powerful than a resume:

A story.

Your story isn't about marks, medals, or model answers.

It's about choices you made, challenges you overcame, and the values you lived by when no one was watching.

"Selection boards don't choose perfect people.

They choose authentic personalities with purposeful stories."

Let's help you discover, structure, and share your story—the one that reflects your real potential as an officer.

Why Your Story Matters

At every stage—TAT, SDT, Interview, GTO tasks—your responses are pieces of a bigger puzzle: who you are, and what drives you.

Your story:

- Builds trust with assessors

- Shows your self-awareness

- Communicates your values, resilience, and leadership

- Makes you memorable

The 3 Elements of a Strong Personal Story

1. Background – Where You Come From

- Family, environment, influences

- Upbringing values, key moments of childhood

- What shaped your early mindset

2. Breakthroughs – What Changed You

- A challenge you faced

- A failure that taught you

- A role you took up and grew into

- A turning point where you became more responsible or self-aware

3. Beliefs & Purpose – What You Stand For

- Why you want to join the Armed Forces

- What values you live by

- What kind of leader you aim to be

- Your vision for your life and contribution

"Every officer has a reason beyond the uniform.

Your story should reflect that reason—genuinely."

How to Craft Your Story (Step-by-Step)

Step 1: Reflect

Ask yourself:

- What was the toughest moment in my life—and what did I learn?

- What am I most proud of that doesn't involve a prize?

- Who do I want to become—and why?

Step 2: Map It

Use this simple framework:

Section	Example
Background	"I come from a small town where values were everything…"
Challenge	"In Class 10, I failed to qualify for [X]… but that failure made me…"
Transformation	"That phase taught me responsibility, and I began leading group projects…"
Purpose	"Today, I want to serve in the armed forces not just for a career, but to live a life of contribution…"

Step 3: Practice, Don't Memorize

You don't need to say your story the same way every time.

But you must be clear about who you are and why you're here.

Where to Use Your Story

SSB Segment	How It Shows
Interview	Through answers to personal, purpose-based, and situational questions
Self-Description Test	When writing how you see yourself and want to grow
Blank TAT Slide	To share a real-life story of growth or leadership
Lecturette	As a relatable anecdote to support your topic
Command Task	Through your quiet confidence and decision-making

What Your Story Shouldn't Be

- A list of achievements

- A memorized speech

- A victim's tale or blame game

- Overly dramatic or unrealistic

- Borrowed from someone else's life

"Your story isn't what happened to you.

It's what you did with what happened."

So own it. Shape it. Share it—with honesty, humility, and pride.

Because when the board sees a clear story of growth, values, and purpose,

they don't see a candidate.

They see an officer in the making.

10.2. Most Common and Unexpected Questions

Prepare for the Known. Stay Calm for the Surprising.

The SSB Interview isn't just a series of questions. It's a conversation designed to uncover your core personality—your mindset, awareness, leadership, and ability to respond under pressure.

Some questions are expected. Some catch you off guard. But the key is this:

"Don't aim to impress.

Respond with presence, honesty, and clarity."

Let's break down the most common questions you must prepare— and a few unexpected ones that test your mindset and spontaneity.

Most Common SSB Interview Questions

Personal & Background

- Tell me about yourself.

- Why do you want to join the Armed Forces?

- What are your strengths and weaknesses?

- Tell me something about your family.

- Who is your role model and why?

Tip: Keep it real, structured, and specific. Avoid long, generic replies.

Education & Career

- Why did you choose this stream/course?

- What were your favorite and least favorite subjects?

- Why did your marks drop in XYZ year/subject?

- What have you learned from your college life/work experience?

- Why switch from engineering/commerce to defence?

Tip: Own your choices. Show learning, not regret.

Armed Forces Awareness

- What do you know about the NDA/CDS/OTA/IMA/AFA?

- Who is the current Army/Navy/Air Force Chief?

- What are the latest defence procurements or operations?

- What is the rank structure in your preferred force?

- Difference between leadership and management?

Tip: Read defence news, stay updated, and revise your basics.

Hobbies, Sports & Interests

- What do you do in your free time?

- Which sport do you play and what have you learned from it?

- Which books have you read recently?

- Tell me about your favorite movie and why.

- How do you spend your Sundays?

Tip: Mention real hobbies you consistently pursue. Be prepared to answer follow-up questions.

Current Affairs & Opinions

- What are your views on social media?

- How can India improve education/health/defence sectors?

- Should India focus more on military or diplomacy?

- Your opinion on recent international conflicts or events?

Tip: Balance facts with personal opinion. Be logical, not emotional.

Situational & Psychological

- What would you do if a friend betrays your trust?

- What if you're not recommended this time?

- How do you handle failure, conflict, or criticism?

- How would you lead a team that's not listening to you?

Tip: Show calm, responsibility, and self-reflection.

Unexpected & Tricky Questions (With Smart Response Tips)

Question	Why It's Asked	How to Respond
You have low marks. Why should we select you?	To check self-awareness and recovery mindset	Acknowledge it, explain the reason, and highlight what you've done to grow

Tell me a lie.	To test spontaneity and reaction	Smile, keep it light and humorous—e.g., "I don't love morning PT!"
Who's better—your father or mother?	Tests emotional intelligence	Show balance and appreciation for both roles
Rate yourself out of 10.	Confidence vs arrogance check	Be honest—"7/10. I'm growing, and I'm aware of what I'm working on."
Convince me why I should recommend you.	Self-confidence and articulation	Express calmly: "Because I'm aware, committed, and ready to serve with clarity and consistency."

Bonus Prep: Rapid-Fire Round

You may be asked a series of 20–50 rapid-fire questions in one go (especially about your PIQ details).

Example:

"What's your favorite food, last 5 books you read, 3 best friends' names, their hobbies, your daily routine, the last movie you saw, your 3 strengths, 3 weaknesses…"

Tips:

- Stay calm. Don't panic if you miss a few.

- Listen carefully.

- Answer fast, honestly, and confidently.

"The SSB Interview is not about perfect answers.

It's about presenting your truth—with thought, balance, and clarity."

So prepare well—but stay real.

Expect surprises—but stay steady.

And above all, let your clarity, character, and commitment speak louder than any rehearsed line.

10.3. Handling Tricky Situations with Grace

Because Leadership Shines Brightest in Difficult Moments

At the SSB—and in life—not everything will go your way.

There will be moments when you're caught off guard, challenged, questioned, or even misunderstood.

What matters most in these moments is not your answer.

It's your attitude, awareness, and ability to stay composed.

"Grace under pressure is the hallmark of a future officer."

Let's explore how to handle tricky, unexpected, or challenging situations with clarity and calm confidence.

What Is a Tricky Situation at SSB?

It could be:

- A confusing or uncomfortable question in the interview

- A heated moment in group discussion

- A mistake during GTO tasks

- A difficult choice in psychology tests

- An emotional dip during the 5-day process

It's not about "right" or "wrong."

It's about how you respond, not just react.

The 3C Formula for Graceful Handling

1. Calmness

Pause. Breathe. Smile. Create a second of space between the situation and your response.

"Stability in emotion is strength in motion."

2. Clarity

Understand the intention behind the situation.

What is really being tested—your knowledge, your honesty, or your composure?

"Respond to what is asked—not what you fear is being judged."

3. Character

Stick to your values. Show maturity, empathy, and ownership.

"When in doubt, choose authenticity over performance."

Real Examples of Tricky SSB Situations (And How to Handle Them)

Situation	Graceful Way to Handle
You forgot what you wrote in TAT/SDT	Smile and say, "Sir, I don't remember the exact lines, but I can share the essence if you'd like."

You're asked a personal or uncomfortable question	Take a moment, stay respectful, and say, "That's a difficult one—but I'll try to answer honestly."
Someone in GD is shouting or interrupting	Don't react emotionally. Wait, then say, "Let's give everyone a chance to speak."
You trip or make a mistake in GTO task	Get up, laugh it off, and continue with spirit. Show resilience, not regret.
You don't know the answer to a question	Say: "I'm not aware of that right now, but I'd love to read up on it after this."
You're criticized or challenged by a fellow aspirant	Respond with calm logic, or simply say, "Let's agree to disagree and move forward."

Mindsets to Carry into Tricky Moments

- I'm not here to be perfect. I'm here to be present.

- Mistakes don't define me—how I bounce back does.

- I can be honest and still strong.

- I control my response—even if I can't control the situation.

Daily Practice to Build Grace

1. Journal your emotional triggers – What makes you angry, nervous, or defensive?

2. Role-play tricky questions with a friend

3. Practice pausing before answering

4. Watch confident leaders speak under pressure (debates, military leaders, interviews)

5. Reflect on how you handled conflict or mistakes in your past

"Tricky situations are not traps.

They're invitations—to show who you truly are under pressure."

So smile. Stay steady. Respond with presence.

That's how leaders—and officers—are remembered and respected.

10.4. Body Language and Confidence

Because You Speak Even Before You Speak

At the SSB, long before your words are judged, your body has already spoken.

Your posture, gestures, eye contact, and energy reveal volumes about your mindset, confidence, and leadership potential.

The best part?

You don't need to fake it. You just need to align your inner clarity with your outer calm.

"Confidence isn't about being loud. It's about being grounded, alert, and authentic."

Why Body Language Matters at SSB

Across all tasks—interview, GD, GTO tasks, Lecturette, psych tests—the assessors are observing your non-verbal cues just as much as your answers.

They look for signs of:

- Nervousness or calmness

- Fakeness or authenticity

- Aggression or composure

- Arrogance or humility

- Leadership or insecurity

"Your body language is your first impression—and your silent recommendation letter."

Top Body Language Practices for SSB

1. Posture = Presence

- Sit and stand upright, not stiff

- Shoulders relaxed, chest open

- Avoid leaning too much or slouching

"Your posture should say: I'm calm, prepared, and ready to engage."

2. Eye Contact = Confidence

- Make steady eye contact—not staring, not avoiding

- In group tasks, scan the group gently while speaking

- In interviews, look at the officer, then pause and reflect if needed

3. Facial Expression = Composure

- Keep a gentle, natural expression

- Smile politely when needed—don't fake enthusiasm

- Don't show visible frustration, fear, or panic (especially during tricky moments)

4. Hands & Gestures = Clarity

- Use open gestures (not crossed arms or pointing fingers)

- Avoid fidgeting with pens, clothes, or chairs

- During Lecturette or interview, use light hand movements to support your words

5. Feet = Grounding

- Don't tap your foot or shift constantly

- Plant your feet slightly apart when standing—it creates instant stability

Mind-Body Connection

Your mind influences your body, and your body feeds back to your mind.

So if you're nervous:

- Pause and breathe—deeply, 3–5 slow breaths

- Open your posture—chest up, arms free

- Smile gently—even when unsure

These small adjustments create a chemical shift—you'll feel calmer, clearer, and more in control.

"Leadership doesn't begin in the voice.

It begins in the breath, the body, and the inner stillness."

Common Body Language Mistakes to Avoid

Mistake	What It Signals
Slouching	Lack of energy or confidence
Fidgeting	Nervousness or lack of control
Crossing arms	Closed mindset or defensiveness
Avoiding eye contact	Dishonesty or fear
Speaking too fast	Anxiety or memorized speech
Overacting gestures	Drama or inauthenticity

Simple Daily Confidence Routine

1. Mirror Practice (2 mins daily):

   o Practice posture, greeting, smiling, and introducing yourself

2. Lecturette Walkthrough (3 mins):

- o Record yourself speaking and review your gestures and expression

3. Body Language Reset (Anytime):

- o Pause, straighten up, take 3 deep breaths—before entering any room or task

"Confidence is not about having all the answers.

It's about being present, steady, and ready—whatever comes your way."

So let your body reflect your preparation.

Let your energy reflect your intention.

And let your presence speak of the officer you are becoming.

Chapter 11

11. Day 5: The Final Conference

Where the Board Confirms What You've Already Shown

The Final Day.

The moment every SSB aspirant looks forward to—and silently fears.

The Conference is when all three assessors—the Interviewing Officer (IO), the Group Testing Officer (GTO), and the Psychologist—sit together to decide one thing:

"Is this candidate ready to wear the uniform, be trained, and grow into an officer?"

It's not a test. It's a final confirmation.

By Day 5, 90% of your assessment is already done.

Now, they're looking for clarity, consistency, and composure.

What Is the SSB Conference?

- Each candidate is called in one by one

- The board (9–15 officers) will be seated formally

- One of them (usually your IO) will speak to you

- Duration: Usually 1–3 minutes

- A few questions may be asked—some serious, some casual

Don't let the atmosphere overwhelm you.

You're not there to prove anything—just to show up as your natural self.

What Actually Happens in the Conference Room?

Before you enter, the assessors discuss your performance:

- Did your personality remain consistent across psych, GTO, and interview?

- Do your OLQs (Officer-Like Qualities) show a strong foundation?

- Are there any doubts, gaps, or contradictions?

If all assessors agree—your recommendation or non-recommendation is usually decided.

If there's a borderline case, they may use the conference interaction to tilt the scale.

Questions You May Be Asked

Common Questions:

- How was your SSB experience?

- Which task did you enjoy the most?

- Which task was difficult and why?

- What did you learn in these five days?

- How do you feel right now?

Borderline Case Questions:

- If not selected, what will you do next?

- What improvement would you make if you come again?

- What's your backup plan?

- How would your friends describe you in one word?

There's no "perfect" answer here. They're checking your honesty, maturity, and emotional balance.

Tips for a Great Conference Impression

1. Walk In with Confidence

- Knock gently, ask for permission

- Greet everyone with "Good Morning Sirs/Ma'ams"

- Stand straight, smile slightly, and stay composed

2. Answer Calmly and Briefly

- No need to narrate long stories

- Speak with presence, not pressure

3. Show Gratefulness, Not Desperation

"I've enjoyed every part of this experience. It's helped me understand myself better."

This shows maturity—even if you're not recommended, you walk out stronger and wiser.

4. If You're Asked About Failure

- Acknowledge it gracefully

- Share your learning

- Show intent to improve and return

"The conference is not the climax—it's the conclusion.

And your confidence, humility, and calmness are the final message you send to the board."

So step in with:

- Gratitude for the journey

- Confidence in your truth

- And peace in your heart—knowing you gave it your best

Because whether you're recommended or not...

You just spent five days becoming more aware, more grounded, and more ready—for life, leadership, and beyond.

SSB Aspirant's Core Practices

Build What the Board Looks For—From the Inside Out

The SSB doesn't select based on memorized answers or rehearsed confidence.

It selects based on consistent behavior, rooted in who you are—not who you pretend to be.

To succeed, your focus should be on developing qualities that naturally flow into every task — be it a psychological test, group task, interview, or command situation.

Let's build your inner foundation using the three essential virtues:

CLARITY – The Power to Think Clearly and Act Decisively

Reflect daily: Ask yourself, "What did I do well today? Where did I hesitate? Why?"

Journal regularly to improve self-awareness and organize your thoughts.

Practice structuring your thinking: in any task or conversation, follow a format (situation → understanding → solution).

Train with mock psych tests (TAT/WAT/SRT) under time pressure — but always review what your answers say about you.

Avoid mental clutter: Be present in every moment—listen deeply before responding.

Simplify your speech and writing: remove unnecessary words; speak with purpose.

CHARACTER – The Foundation of Leadership

Take responsibility—don't wait to be told what's right. Own your words, actions, and decisions.

Support others even when it doesn't benefit you — this is real team spirit.

Stay calm under pressure—when stuck in a task or decision, pause, breathe, and think.

Follow the rules willingly—not to impress the GTO, but to show integrity.

Show initiative—don't wait for permission to act, especially in group tasks.

Respect everyone—from fellow aspirants to support staff. Character shows in small interactions.

COMMUNICATION – The Bridge Between Thought and Action

Speak with structure: Always use a simple flow — intro, body, conclusion.

Practice Lecturette daily: Random topics, 3 minutes, clear points. Record and review.

In group discussions, listen more than you speak — but speak when it adds value.

Be concise: Say more with fewer words. Avoid fillers.

Use examples, stories, and data: These make your points believable and relatable.

Practice eye contact and confident posture in all interactions—not just in tests.

How to Make These Practices Automatic

Daily Habit	What It Builds
10 minutes of mindfulness	Calmness, clarity, focus
1 page of journaling	Self-awareness, reflective thinking
Random Lecturette practice	Fluency, structured speech
Helping 1 person daily	Compassion, initiative
Physical fitness routine	Energy, discipline, presence
Reading (biographies, defense books)	Values, purpose, officer-like thinking
Weekly group discussion with peers	Idea exchange, team voice, adaptability

You don't have to prepare for each task individually.

Instead, build one personality that responds to all tasks with:

Clarity of thought

Strength of character

Effectiveness in communication

"When these traits become part of who you are, the SSB doesn't feel like a test—it becomes a natural expression of your best self."

11.1. What Really Happens Behind the Doors

The Truth About How You're Assessed—Silently, Systematically, and Fairly

After days of physical effort, group tasks, interviews, and psychology tests, many aspirants walk away wondering:

"What exactly are they discussing behind those closed doors? What do they see that I don't?"

Let's pull back the curtain—without mystery or myth.

This chapter isn't just about SSB secrets. It's about helping you understand the depth, dignity, and fairness behind the process.

The Real Purpose of the SSB

The SSB isn't designed to select perfect candidates.

It's designed to identify raw officer potential—someone who:

- Can lead in uncertainty

- Can think clearly under pressure

- Can live with integrity

- Can grow into a capable officer through training

"They're not choosing the most talented—they're choosing the most trainable."

Who Sits Behind the Table?

There are three core assessors:

1. Interviewing Officer (IO) – Evaluates your personality through your interaction

2. Group Testing Officer (GTO) – Observes you in group dynamics and physical tasks

3. Psychologist – Studies your mind, thoughts, and inner wiring through psych tests

All three assess you independently.

They do not discuss your case until Day 5, during the final conference.

What They Look For Collectively

They try to answer a single question:

"Is this person suitable to be trained as an officer?"

They look for OLQs (Officer-Like Qualities) like:

- Initiative

- Responsibility

- Team spirit

- Emotional stability

- Effective intelligence

- Courage

- Self-confidence

- Social adaptability

But they're not looking for textbook answers.

They're looking for patterns of behavior—real, consistent traits.

How They Cross-Check Your Consistency

Area	What's Checked
Psych Tests	Inner mindset, instinctive thought patterns
Interview	External personality, clarity, awareness

GTO	Leadership in action, group cooperation, presence

If all three see a common thread of OLQs—you are likely to be recommended.

If there's contradiction (e.g., confident in interview but unstable in psych), they dig deeper.

Behind Closed Doors on Day 5: The Conference

Here's what really happens:

- All three assessors sit in the room with your files open

- Each shares their independent observations

- They compare notes—does the picture align or conflict?

- If all agree → clear recommendation or non-recommendation

- If borderline → the IO may ask you a few more questions in the conference to help tip the decision

"It's a collective call—not a judgment. They genuinely want you to succeed, but only if you are ready."

What Might Tilt the Decision?

- Consistent OLQs across tests

- Honest and reflective responses

- Balanced attitude (not overconfident or self-doubting)

- Potential to improve during training

- Maturity in handling pressure, feedback, and teamwork

What Doesn't Work (Even if It Seems to)

- Over-coached or rehearsed answers

- Pretending to be someone you're not

- Memorizing stories or trying to "crack" the tests

- Performing well in one area but failing in the others

- Faking confidence without internal clarity

"What happens behind the doors is not about marks.

It's about minds, maturity, and momentum."

So don't try to manipulate the process.

Trust it. Walk in as a learner. Live the OLQs instead of listing them.

And if you do that with awareness, effort, and truth—

then what happens behind the doors will reflect what's already shining within you.

11.2. How the Board Evaluates You

Not on Perfection—But on Potential, Consistency, and Character

Most aspirants believe the SSB is about cracking the test.

But in truth, it's about revealing the person behind the performance.

The assessors—Interviewing Officer (IO), Group Testing Officer (GTO), and Psychologist—don't select you based on marks, tricks, or fluency.

They select you based on how well you reflect the Officer-Like Qualities (OLQs) consistently across the 5-day process.

Let's break down exactly how you are evaluated—so you can stop guessing, and start growing.

The 3-Dimensional Evaluation Process

The board evaluates you through three different lenses:

Assessor	Tool	What They Evaluate
Psychologist	TAT, WAT, SRT, SDT	Inner personality, values, mental pattern
Interviewing Officer (IO)	Personal interview	Awareness, logic, emotional balance, decision-making
Group Testing Officer (GTO)	GD, PGT, GPE, CT, IO, etc.	Group dynamics, action-based leadership, cooperation

Each assessor gives a separate and independent opinion.

They do not influence each other before the final conference on Day 5.

There are 15 OLQs that the board is trained to evaluate. These are grouped into 4 categories.

You're not expected to be perfect in all 15.

But a balanced, authentic personality with observable potential in these areas is what the board looks for.

Consistency Across Assessments = Key

The final decision is often based on:

- How consistent your qualities are across all tasks

- Whether your inner thinking (psychology) matches your spoken behavior (interview) and team actions (GTO)

- How well you reflect the raw potential to grow into a good officer through training

Evaluation in Each Assessment Tool

Area	What the Assessor Looks For
Psychology (TAT, WAT, SRT, SDT)	Instinctive thinking, values, self-image, reaction to pressure
Interview	Communication, honesty, awareness, decision-making, life experience
GTO Tasks	Leadership in group, participation, problem-solving, calmness, energy, group contribution

What Helps You Get Recommended

- Natural leadership, not forced

- Self-awareness and honesty about strengths and weaknesses

- Team-first attitude, not self-promotion

- Clear thinking under pressure

- Ability to adapt and bounce back from failure

- A consistent personality across all test formats

What Prevents Recommendation

- Contradiction between psychology, interview, and GTO behavior

- Inauthentic or "coached" responses

- Dominating or passive behavior in group tasks

- Lack of initiative or awareness

- Nervous breakdown under pressure

- Superficial motivation for joining forces ("for uniform," "glory," etc.)

Self-Evaluation Questions

Reflect on the following before and after your SSB:

1. Do I take initiative without seeking attention?

2. Can I think clearly when put on the spot?

3. Do I listen and include others in group settings?

4. Am I emotionally balanced in tough moments?

5. Do my actions reflect my values?

"The board does not select the best speaker or strongest athlete.

They select the one who shows the clarity, character, and calmness to grow into a leader."

So stop performing. Start becoming.

You are not evaluated on your show—you are evaluated on your substance.

11.3. When You're Not Selected: What's Next?

Because One Result Doesn't Define Your Worth—Your Response Does

Not everyone gets recommended.

Even brilliant, sincere, and high-potential candidates walk out of the SSB with a polite handshake and that one word:

"Not Recommended."

It hurts. Of course it does.

You gave your all—heart, sweat, discipline.

But this moment doesn't mean you're not good enough.

It simply means—you're not ready yet.

"SSB is not a rejection. It's reflection.

Not an end. Just a bend in the path."

Let's talk about what to do after SSB, especially when the result says "try again."

First: What This Result Really Means

It does *not* mean:

- You are a failure

- You lack leadership

- You should give up on your dream

It *does* mean:

- There are areas where your personality needs alignment

- The board did not see sufficient consistency in OLQs

- You now have feedback in disguise—a direction to grow

Reflect Before You React

After the result:

- Pause. Breathe. Journal.

- Don't rush to blame the system, the board, or yourself

- Ask:

"Where did I feel least confident?"

"Was I being real—or rehearsed?"

"Where can I become stronger—in mind, body, or expression?"

"The SSB shows you not your weakness—but your next chapter of growth."

Rebuild with Strategy, Not Emotion

1. Review Your Performance Holistically

Ask yourself:

- Was my psychology test honest and natural?

- Did I show calm, clarity, and contribution in GTO tasks?

- Did I handle the interview with self-awareness and truth?

2. Work on Alignment

Often, the issue is not lack of quality—but lack of consistency across tests.

Your goal: Same personality across psychology, interview, and GTO.

Prepare for the Comeback

1. Polish Your OLQs

Use an OLQ checklist. Practice expressing leadership, empathy, initiative, and calmness in daily life.

2. Practice Mindfulness & Journaling

Improve self-awareness. Understand how you think, respond, and grow.

3. Mock Interview + Group Practice

Seek feedback not from flatterers, but from honest mentors.

4. Set a 90-Day Growth Plan

- Mental clarity

- Physical fitness

- Emotional balance

- Current affairs & defence awareness

- Spoken English & confidence

Remember These Truths

- Some great officers were recommended in their 4th or 5th attempt

- You are not racing against others—you are becoming yourself

- A gap between effort and result is not failure. It's foundation.

"Not recommended is not a verdict. It's a review.

One door didn't open—but now you know where your key needs polishing."

So get up. Stand taller. Train wiser.

And come back—not to prove the board wrong, but to prove to yourself that you won't quit on the officer within you.

You're not done. You're just getting better.

PART IV: SUCCEEDING BEYOND THE SSB

Because the Officer Within You Is Not Limited to One Selection Board

Success in life is not defined by one exam, one uniform, or one result.

It's defined by the values you live, the impact you create, and the person you choose to become—day after day.

Whether you are recommended or not, your SSB journey is a gift—because it introduced you to the officer within you.

"The SSB is not the destination.

It's a launchpad—for a life of purpose, courage, and contribution."

Let's talk about how to succeed beyond the SSB—as a leader, a professional, and a human being who lives with clarity and character.

What SSB Teaches You (Even if You Weren't Selected)

- How to handle pressure with calmness

- How to think clearly and act quickly

- How to speak with purpose and listen with empathy

- How to lead without shouting and serve without seeking reward

- How to bounce back from failure with dignity

These are not exam skills.

These are life assets.

Paths Beyond the Parade Ground

If not selected—or if your journey in the forces ends earlier than planned—it's not the end.

You can still live like a leader, serve society, and grow into greatness.

Consider:

- Paramilitary forces / CAPF / Coast Guard

- State or central civil services

- Entrepreneurship with a mission-driven mindset

- Corporate roles needing leadership and resilience

- Education, social impact, or nation-building projects

- Joining defence prep institutions to guide future aspirants

"The spirit of service doesn't need a commission—it just needs conviction."

Redefine Success

Success is not just about stars on your shoulder.

It's about:

- Holding your values when the world tests them

- Speaking the truth when it's easier to stay silent

- Uplifting others when you've just been knocked down

- Choosing contribution over comparison

True Success Sounds Like:

- "I didn't give up."

- "I became better every time life tested me."

- "I helped others grow—no matter what I was going through."

- "I live every day with the mindset of an officer—even if I wear no uniform."

You Are Already Officer Material When...

- You lead your family with kindness

- You help your friends without ego

- You stay disciplined without being watched

- You chase excellence, not applause

- You choose growth—even when it's hard

"You carry the uniform in your values long before you wear it on your shoulders."

Final Word: This Is Your Victory

If you've walked the SSB path:

- You are braver than most

- You are more self-aware than many

- And you are more prepared for life than you realize

So wear your experience with pride.

Keep your mind sharp, your spirit humble, and your goals high.

And wherever life takes you, carry the officer within you.

Because the world needs more humans who think like leaders,

act with responsibility,

and live with quiet strength.

And that's exactly what you've become.

Chapter 12

12. TRAINING AT DIFFERENT OFFICERS TRAINING ACADEMIES

The Making of an Officer—Across Every Uniform, in Every Terrain

Becoming an officer in the Indian Armed Forces is not just about passing an exam or clearing the SSB.

It's about undergoing transformational training—the kind that builds not just strength, but character, clarity, and courage.

This training happens in some of the most iconic institutions of India, where the spirit of service meets the art of leadership.

Let's take you through what it truly means to train like a warrior, think like a leader, and live like an officer—across the Army, Navy, and Air Force training academies.

1. Indian Military Academy (IMA), Dehradun

For: Permanent Commission (Army)

Duration: 18 months (Direct Entry) | 12 months (from NDA)

Training Focus:

- Tactical warfare, fieldcraft, weapon handling

- Physical endurance and obstacle courses

- Leadership and command training

- Combined arms warfare, map reading, battle drills

- Ethical and moral development through service traditions

- The final Passing Out Parade at Chetwode Building is among the most iconic military ceremonies in India.

2. Officer Training Academy (OTA), Chennai & Gaya

For: Short Service Commission (Men & Women)

Duration: 49 weeks

Training Focus:

- Compact, intense leadership training

- Emphasis on time-bound combat readiness

- Physical training, battle craft, firing, and drills

- Personality grooming and spoken English

- Emotional resilience and mental stamina

Unique Highlights:

- OTA produces battle-ready officers in under a year

- Cadets from varied academic and professional backgrounds

- Women cadets undergo equal training with pride and precision

3. Indian Naval Academy (INA), Ezhimala

For: Naval Officers (NDA, 10+2 BTech, Graduate Entries)

Duration: 4 years (BTech + Naval training) or 22 weeks to 1 year (Graduate Entry)

Training Focus:

- Seamanship, navigation, and marine warfare

- Swimming, rowing, and survival training at sea

- Academic curriculum + naval operations

- Parade, sailing regattas, and maritime law

Unique Highlights:

- Located on the Arabian Sea coast in Kerala

- India's largest military academy by area

- Combines engineering knowledge with leadership training for modern naval warfare

4. Air Force Academy (AFA), Dundigal

For: Flying, Technical & Ground Duty Officers

Duration: ~74 weeks (Flying Branch) | Varies for others

Training Focus:

- Ground training + simulator-based flying

- Air combat tactics, air navigation, aviation law

- Rigorous academics, physical fitness, and aero-medical training

- Psychological preparation for high-pressure air missions

Unique Highlights:

- Cadets train with Kiran Mk II and PC-7 aircraft

- High discipline, scientific approach, and precision

- Prepares fighter pilots, engineers, and leaders in aerospace warfare

5. National Defence Academy (NDA), Khadakwasla

For: Cadets selected for Army, Navy, Air Force (Joint training)

Duration: 3 years (graduation + military foundation)

Followed by: 1–1.5 years at respective service academies (IMA/INA/AFA)

Training Focus:

- Joint training across services (Army, Navy, Air Force)

- Academic degree + military grooming

- Emphasis on brotherhood, drill, and multi-domain awareness

- Builds tri-service understanding and lifelong bonds

Unique Highlights:

- World's first tri-service military academy

- Cadets go on to become top generals, admirals, and air marshals

- Motto: *"Service Before Self"*

The Core of All Academies: The Officer Spirit

Despite the difference in uniforms, terrains, weapons, and technologies, all academies teach the same core values:

- Discipline without supervision

- Service before self

- Courage with compassion

- Tactical clarity under pressure

- Respect for subordinates and pride in the nation

"The uniform may be stitched in cloth.

But the officer is stitched in sweat, struggle, and silent transformation."

Whether you're training under the Himalayan mist of Dehradun, the salty breeze of Ezhimala, the winds of Dundigal, or the drill grounds of Chennai—

you're not just learning how to fight.

You're learning how to lead with integrity, live with honour, and serve with purpose.

That's what the academies build.

That's who you are becoming.

12.1. First Day in Uniform

Because You Don't Just Wear It—You Become It

You've cleared the SSB.

You've endured months of mental, emotional, and physical transformation at the academy.

And then one day, it arrives—your first day in uniform.

It isn't just fabric stitched with buttons and badges.

It's a symbol of every sacrifice, every sleepless night, every failure you rose from, and every dream you never gave up on.

"The first day you wear the uniform is the day you stop being a civilian—and start living as a soldier, a guardian, a leader."

The Moment You Put It On

The feeling is unlike anything you've experienced before.

You look in the mirror—not at your clothes, but at your character.

You feel:

- Taller, though your height hasn't changed

- Quieter, though your mind is at peace

- Stronger, though your hands may still tremble

- Humbled, by the weight of responsibility it carries

This isn't pride born out of ego.

It's pride born from belonging—to something greater than yourself.

What the Uniform Represents

Each element of your uniform carries meaning:

Symbol	Meaning
Name Tag	You no longer hide—you represent yourself, fully.
Unit Patch / Academy Crest	You are part of a legacy larger than one lifetime.
Stars / Stripes / Ranks	You lead not for power, but with purpose.
Shine of the Boots	A reminder that glory is built from ground-level discipline.
Olive, White, or Blue	Each colour whispers the same message—*India first.*

The Inner Shift

It's not just a change of dress. It's a shift in identity:

- You now walk with accountability

- You speak with measured confidence

- You treat others with respect—regardless of their status

- You hold yourself to a higher standard, even when no one's watching

"Your choices become national. Your words carry weight.

Your actions inspire—or disappoint. You are now seen—not just as a person, but as a protector."

What You Hear on Day One

- "Welcome to the brotherhood/sisterhood."

- "You've earned it. Now uphold it."

- "The nation sees you differently now—so must you."

- And sometimes, just a silent salute from a senior—that says it all.

What You Feel Inside

- A quiet rush of emotion—tears, pride, purpose

- Memories of parents, mentors, friends who supported you

- A sense of belonging to something sacred

- And most of all, a promise you make to yourself:

"I will honour this uniform. Not just today—but every day."

"Your first day in uniform isn't the end of a dream—it's the beginning of a new duty."

So wear it not just on your body, but in your spirit.

Don't let the shine blind you—let it remind you.

You've become more than a cadet, a student, or a citizen.

You've become an officer-in-the-making.

And the journey has only just begun.

12.2. Mental and Physical Transformation

Because Becoming an Officer Is a Transformation—Not a Transaction

Joining the armed forces isn't about learning to march or handle a rifle.

It's about becoming someone who thinks clearer, feels deeper, leads stronger, and stands taller—in every situation, under every pressure.

What begins as an aspirant's dream slowly transforms into a warrior's mindset and a leader's presence.

And this journey—across your days in preparation, training, and academy life—is nothing less than a complete mental and physical transformation.

"They don't just build your muscles.

They rewire your mind, rebuild your will, and reintroduce you to your best self."

Mental Transformation: Shaping the Officer Mindset

1. From Hesitation to Clarity

You stop second-guessing. You start making clear, confident decisions—even under pressure.

2. From Excuses to Ownership

No more "It's not my fault." Instead, you take full responsibility for actions, outcomes, and effort.

3. From Emotion to Emotional Control

You don't stop feeling. You learn to channel your emotions without letting them control your responses.

4. From Comparison to Contribution

You stop trying to be better than others—and focus on making others better through your presence.

5. From Comfort Zone to Challenge Zone

You learn to seek discomfort, because every stretch makes you stronger.

"The real battlefield is the mind—and officers are trained to win it first."

Physical Transformation: Becoming Battle-Ready

1. Strength with Stamina

Obstacle courses, daily PT, long runs, BPET tests—you don't just build strength, you build sustainable power.

2. Discipline in the Body Clock

Your body learns to wake before the sun, eat what's needed (not what's liked), and perform at its peak on demand.

3. Injury Becomes Instruction

Sprains and soreness don't stop you—they teach you recovery, resilience, and respect for your limits.

4. Drill Sharpens the Nerves

Marching isn't just physical—it's mental rehearsal of focus, alertness, and alignment with a team.

5. Combat Readiness

You're not trained for stage performance—you're trained for real-life battle conditions with minimal error tolerance.

The Fusion: Where Mind and Body Align

True transformation is when:

- Your body obeys your mind

- Your mind serves your mission

- And your mission drives your life

"Discipline outside. Decisiveness inside.

And a quiet confidence that radiates through everything you do."

Before vs After: You Won't Recognize Yourself

Before OTA/IMA/AFA/INA	After Training
Wants success	Lives purpose
Scared of failure	Uses failure as fuel
Seeks motivation	Builds daily discipline
Follows orders	Gives direction with calm authority

Dreams of uniform	Becomes worthy of it

"The making of an officer is not about adding stars to your shoulders.

It's about removing doubts from your mind, weakness from your body, and fear from your heart."

So if you feel pain in training, confusion in preparation, or fear in the journey—

smile.

It means your transformation has begun.

Keep going.

Because the world doesn't just need more officers.

It needs transformed individuals who live with courage, clarity, and character—just like you.

12.3. Discipline, Brotherhood, and Responsibility

The Three Pillars That Forge the Soul of an Officer

Every great soldier is built on three timeless foundations:

Discipline, Brotherhood, and Responsibility.

These aren't just values whispered in academy speeches.

They are lived daily, tested under pressure, and etched into the character of every man and woman who dares to wear the uniform.

Let's explore why these three are not just military principles—but the very core of the officer's life.

1. Discipline: The Backbone of Leadership

In the academy, discipline is the first lesson and the last habit.

You rise at 4:30 AM. You make your bed with precision. You march, run, plan, and execute—not because someone is watching, but because that's who you've become.

"Discipline is doing what is right, even when it's hard, even when it's unseen."

What Discipline Teaches You:

- Self-respect through consistency

- Time mastery—you learn to beat the clock, not chase it

- Decision-making clarity—because a trained mind doesn't panic

- Leadership through example, not instruction

In war or in peace, in uniform or beyond—a disciplined life is a successful life.

2. Brotherhood: More Than Friendship—It's Trust Without Conditions

In training, you share food, punishment, victories, and breakdowns.

You tie each other's shoelaces when one's too injured to bend.

You push each other through the last lap when motivation fades.

You laugh together. You cry silently.

And slowly, you stop saying "I"—and start saying "we."

"Brotherhood is when your life matters more to me than mine."

What Brotherhood Builds:

- Team-first attitude in every decision

- Shared sacrifice, which strengthens moral fiber

- Unbreakable trust, forged through hardship

- Emotional strength—you're never truly alone

This bond transcends religion, caste, language, and ego.

You don't choose your brothers—you earn them.

3. Responsibility: The Officer's Real Rank

Ranks can be worn on the shoulder.

Responsibility is carried on the soul.

Whether you lead a unit, carry a rifle, or stand guard at midnight—your decisions impact lives.

One wrong call can cost lives. One right stand can save a mission.

That's why officers are trained to think, act, and lead with maturity, not mood.

"Responsibility is when you stop blaming and start owning."

What Responsibility Demands:

- Moral courage—doing what's right even when it's unpopular

- Clarity in chaos—leaders cannot afford confusion

- Respect for duty—without shortcuts or show

- Readiness to sacrifice—for men, mission, and country

It's responsibility that transforms a cadet into an officer, and an officer into a legend.

How They All Work Together

Value	Fuels	Forms
Discipline	Focus & Reliability	Inner Strength
Brotherhood	Unity & Trust	Social Stability
Responsibility	Integrity & Action	Moral Leadership

These aren't separate traits. They're woven into one fabric—the uniform you wear with pride.

"An officer is not born in front of the mirror.

He or she is forged in early wakeups, shared struggles, and choices made in silence."

So live disciplined.

Stand by your brothers and sisters.

And carry your responsibilities with quiet strength.

That's not just how officers are made.

That's how they live—every single day.

Chapter 13

13. YOUR INNER COMMISSION: CHARACTER FOR LIFE

Because the True Officer Is Commissioned in the Heart—Long Before the Rank

Clearing the SSB, entering the academy, and earning the uniform are monumental milestones.

But there is a commission even more sacred than the one the President of India signs.

It's the inner commission—when you decide, deeply and consciously,

"From this day forward, I will live like an officer... even without a badge."

This is not about a selection result.

It's about a commitment to character, courage, and contribution—for life.

What Is Your Inner Commission?

It's the quiet moment when you realize:

- Discipline is not a rule—it's your rhythm

- Integrity is not imposed—it's your identity

- Service is not a duty—it's your calling

- Leadership is not a title—it's your truth

"You may or may not wear the uniform.

But the world still needs you to stand for something."

How to Live Your Inner Commission

1. Choose Honour Over Ease

Even when shortcuts are tempting, choose the right path.

Even when no one is watching, hold your standards high.

2. Serve Where You Stand

You don't need a posting to serve.

Help your family. Support your community. Mentor someone younger.

Your contribution starts wherever you are.

3. Lead Without Position

You don't need stars to lead.

Lead by example—in your office, classroom, or street.

Let your clarity and calm influence others.

4. Be Unshakable in Crisis

When things go wrong—don't collapse, don't complain.

Stand up. Take charge. Be the strength others seek.

Your Inner Commission Sounds Like...

- *"I won't blame. I'll act."*

- *"I will speak the truth, respectfully."*

- *"I will do what's right—even when it's not easy."*

- *"I will lift others as I rise."*

This is what makes you officer material—not on paper, but in purpose.

Why It Matters Beyond the SSB

Even if you are not in the armed forces:

- You can be the most disciplined engineer

- The most ethical entrepreneur

- The most dependable teammate

- The most respectful leader in any uniform—civil or camouflaged

Because society needs men and women who carry their character like a commission—proudly and permanently.

"The uniform fades. The salutes stop. The parade ends.

But your inner commission—your truth, your integrity, your impact—lives on."

So take that pledge.

Not for selection, but for transformation.

Not for applause, but for alignment.

Because your greatest rank is not what's stitched on your shoulders.

It's what's engraved in your soul.

13.1. How SSB Prepares You for Any Career

Because Once You Train Like an Officer, You Can Thrive Anywhere

The SSB isn't just a gateway to the armed forces.

It's a masterclass in human potential—one that builds habits, mindsets, and qualities that can empower you in any field, any role, and any future.

Even if you're not selected, your SSB journey leaves you more aware, more capable, and more resilient than ever before.

"SSB doesn't just prepare you to wear the uniform.

It prepares you to lead—with or without one."

The Skills SSB Builds That Every Career Demands

1. Clear Thinking Under Pressure

From rapid-fire interview questions to surprise group tasks—SSB trains you to stay calm and think fast without losing depth.

Useful in: Crisis management, entrepreneurship, high-stakes decision-making.

2. Effective Communication

Whether in GDs, lecturettes, or interviews, you learn to speak:

- With structure, not noise

- With purpose, not panic

- With clarity, not confusion

Useful in: Corporate presentations, client interactions, leadership roles, negotiations.

3. Teamwork & Leadership

GTO tasks teach you to:

- Take initiative

- Listen before leading

- Solve problems as a team

- Motivate without dominance

Useful in: Project teams, startup environments, management roles, and NGO work.

4. Self-Awareness & Emotional Intelligence

Psychology tests like TAT, WAT, SRT, and SDT force you to look within—understand who you are, how you think, and why you act the way you do.

Useful in: Personal growth, emotional maturity, conflict resolution, and relationships.

5. Resilience & Bounce-Back Ability

Not getting recommended? It hurts.

But the very act of preparing again—stronger, wiser, calmer— builds grit that few ever develop.

Useful in: Facing job rejections, career pivots, health setbacks, and life's storms.

How SSB Shapes a Career-Ready Personality

Trait Developed	Career Advantage
Time discipline	Meets deadlines, respects structure
Confidence without arrogance	Builds trust in teams and clients
Clarity of thought	Faster and better decision-making
Adaptability	Thrives in change, uncertainty, and growth
Moral grounding	Makes value-driven choices in tough calls
Initiative	Becomes a self-starter and solution finder

"Every job needs a doer. But great careers are built by thinkers, communicators, and contributors—just like those trained through SSB."

Where SSB Alumni Excel Beyond Defence

Many who train for SSB (or even train at the academy) go on to succeed in:

- Civil services (IAS, IPS, IFS, IRS, etc.)

- Corporate leadership (CEOs, HR heads, management consultants)

- Entrepreneurship (startups with a purpose-driven mindset)

- Education & coaching (influencing the next generation)

- Social impact roles (NGOs, think tanks, development sectors)

"You don't leave the SSB empty-handed—even if you leave without a recommendation."

You leave with:

- Greater clarity

- Deeper character

- Sharper skills

- A blueprint for excellence

So, wherever life takes you next—walk in with your officer-like mindset.

Because that mindset doesn't just clear boards.

It builds beautiful, bold, and meaningful careers.

13.2. Becoming an Officer in Life, Not Just in Rank

Because True Leadership Begins Where the Uniform Ends

The world sees an officer as someone in uniform—with ranks, salutes, and command.

But ask any real leader, and they'll tell you:

"Being an officer is not just a career. It's a calling. A way of life."

You may or may not get commissioned.

You may or may not pass the SSB on your first or even fifth attempt.

But you always have the power to live like an officer—every single day.

What Does It Mean to Be an Officer in Life?

It means choosing values over comfort.

Service over selfishness.

Courage over convenience.

It means:

- Walking with integrity, even when no one is watching

- Leading with empathy, not ego

- Owning your actions, in both success and failure

- Being dependable, even when others give up

- Inspiring others, not by words, but by who you are

"It's not about the stars on your shoulders. It's about the light in your character."

Five Ways to Live Like an Officer—Anywhere, Always

1. Make Discipline Your Identity

Wake up early. Stay accountable.

Master your routine so chaos doesn't master you.

2. Be the Strongest in the Storm

When pressure rises, don't run—rise.

Stay calm, find clarity, and help others breathe.

3. Uplift Those Around You

Lead without title. Serve without spotlight.

Make people feel safe, seen, and supported.

4. Take the Hard Right Over the Easy Wrong

That's what real officers do. Even in civilian life.

You know the line—stand on the side of honour.

5. Keep Growing—Always

Train your body. Sharpen your mind.

Learn. Reflect. Evolve. And then repeat.

The World Needs More Officers

Not just in uniforms.

But in homes, classrooms, companies, streets, startups, and social movements.

- Officers who don't cheat to get ahead.

- Officers who step forward when others step back.

- Officers who raise their families with values.

- Officers who build, not just win.

"If we all choose to live like officers, the world wouldn't need protecting—it would start healing."

Commission Yourself

You don't need anyone's signature to start living like an officer.

You can commission yourself today—with a simple, sacred vow:

"From this moment forward, I will live with honour, clarity, compassion, and courage—

in every role, every decision, every situation."

No one can take that away.

No badge can replace it.

No exam can define it.

Because you are not just aiming for rank.

You are becoming an officer—in life.

13.3. Integrity, Purpose, and Clarity in the Real World

The Officer's Compass for Everyday Life

The world outside the academy doesn't run on drills and parades.

It's chaotic, competitive, often grey, and full of shortcuts.

That's why the true test of an officer-like mindset doesn't happen on the training ground.

It happens in the real world—

Where decisions are tough, temptations are real, and the path of truth is rarely easy.

"You were not trained just to salute, follow, or fight.

You were trained to live with Integrity, Purpose, and Clarity— anywhere."

Let's explore how to carry these three powerful forces into every corner of your personal and professional life.

Integrity: The Courage to Be Consistent

In the real world, you'll face:

- Bribes masked as "rewards"

- Pressure to compromise your values

- Temptation to hide your mistakes

But an officer's soul whispers:

"Do what is right. Even if you stand alone."

How to Practice Integrity Daily:

- Be honest—even when it's inconvenient

- Keep your word—even when it's hard

- Take responsibility—even when it's not your fault

- Speak truthfully—but respectfully

Integrity is not just moral—it's magnetic.

People trust, follow, and respect those who are grounded in truth.

Purpose: The Inner Mission That Never Fades

A job gives you income.

A rank gives you status.

But purpose gives you direction—in your darkest moments and brightest hours.

"When you have a mission, even small tasks feel meaningful."

Questions to Keep Your Purpose Alive:

- Who am I serving through my work or presence?

- Is this choice aligned with my long-term values?

- Would I be proud of this decision 10 years from now?

Whether you're an officer, entrepreneur, teacher, or parent—purpose is what turns routine into service.

Clarity: The Power to Cut Through Confusion

In a world overloaded with information, opinions, and distractions—clarity is leadership.

An officer's training helps you:

- Make quick decisions under pressure

- Filter out noise and stay focused

- Communicate with simplicity and calm authority

How to Build Clarity:

- Reflect daily: What mattered most today?

- Ask better questions: What's the real issue here?

- Simplify your speech: Clear talk reflects clear thought

- Avoid drama: Focus on facts, not emotions

"Clarity is not knowing everything. It's knowing what matters most."

Why These 3 Traits Win in the Real World

Trait	Why It Stands Out	What It Builds
Integrity	Rare in a shortcut-driven world	Trust & long-term respect
Purpose	Gives meaning when motivation fades	Direction & resilience
Clarity	Cuts through chaos	Confidence & impact

These are your inner weapons. No one can take them away.

And they will serve you in every career, every crisis, and every conversation.

"The real battlefield is not at the border.

It's in boardrooms, homes, cities, and hearts—where courage, character, and clarity are in short supply."

So bring your officer soul to this world:

- Walk with integrity

- Act with purpose

- Speak with clarity

That's how you make a difference.

That's how you lead in uniform—or out of it.

That's how you win—not just battles, but respect, impact, and peace.

CONCLUSION

You Were Never Just Preparing for the SSB—You Were Preparing for Life.

By now, you've journeyed through every stage of what it means to be "officer material"—not just in the eyes of the SSB board, but in the deeper, more sacred mission of life itself.

You've seen that success is not about one recommendation letter.

It's about your readiness to lead, your courage to grow, and your clarity to stand for something greater than yourself.

"The SSB doesn't just test your knowledge. It reveals your character."

Whether you are wearing the uniform yet or not, the transformation has already begun.

Because if you've:

Built discipline day after day,

Shaped your mindset with honesty and strength,

And committed to a life of service, responsibility, and authenticity...

Then you are already on your way to becoming the kind of person this world deeply needs—

An officer in life, not just in rank.

Final Commission: A Call to Live Differently

From this point forward, the mission is no longer just about passing a selection board.

It's about:

Being the one others can count on

Standing up when things go wrong

Choosing the hard right over the easy wrong

Living every day with honour, even when no one is watching

Because officership is not a title. It's a testimony.

Keep Growing. Keep Leading. Keep Serving.

You may face rejection.

You may face delays.

You may take longer than expected.

But if you walk this path with integrity, purpose, and courage—

You will never truly fail.

Because you're not just preparing to serve the nation...

You are becoming the kind of citizen that strengthens it.

Thank you for walking through this book with your heart open and your dreams alive.

Now, go forward—

Not to seek greatness,

But to live it.

Every day. Every step.

Because truly...

You're Officer Material.

ACKNOWLEDGEMENTS

To my Uncle, K. Chandran Nair, Retired Master Technician, Hindustan Aeronautics Limited (HAL)—with deepest gratitude and love. You were my pillar of strength, inspiring me to dream of the Armed Forces and supporting me in every possible way—with your wisdom, shelter, food, and even financial help. Your selflessness and belief made my journey into the Services possible.

A special note of gratitude to Lt Col Bala. I don't know much about him, except for the genuine love he carried for teaching SSB aspirants. In the few days I spent learning from him, he left a lifelong impression. The handwritten notes I took during his classes, which I've preserved for years, form the very basis of this book. His impact remains imprinted on every page.

To Brig Atul Mishra, Retd., for writing the foreword to this book and offering valuable suggestions and encouragement. I served under him for a long period, and he consistently pushed me toward excellence. His high standards, sharp eye, and dedication to quality continue to inspire me.

To the officers, instructors, and mentors who trained me, corrected me, and inspired me—during my service, and at every stage of my life —you are the true architects of this book. Your discipline, guidance, and expectations shaped the foundation of who I became.

To my Wife, Cinderella—thank you for believing in me when I doubted myself, for giving me the space I needed to grow, and for standing silently and strongly beside me. Your presence has been my quiet strength.

To my editorial and creative collaborators—editors, proofreaders, designers, and early readers—thank you for your dedication, attention to detail, and care in shaping this work into its best form.

To the reader—whether you are an aspirant, a parent, a mentor, or a dreamer—thank you for picking up this book. May it serve not just as a preparation guide, but as a personal mirror, a moral compass, and a source of courage and clarity on your journey.

To modern technology and AI tools, especially intelligent writing assistants and creative platforms—thank you for offering structure, suggestions, and the ability to organize vast content with clarity. These tools didn't replace my thoughts, but they helped research, refine, reflect, and reframe them, making this book more accessible and relevant to today's generation of aspirants.

To the Supreme Power and all my Divine Guides—thank you for showing me the path, especially during times when I couldn't see it myself. Your unseen hands and sacred presence have guided this journey from within.

ABOUT THE AUTHOR

Veteran. Mentor. Mission-Driven Guide for Tomorrow's Leaders.

Pradeepkumar K. P. is a veteran, engineer, leadership mentor, and personal transformation coach with over 30 years of experience. Throughout his career, he has been dedicated to nurturing individuals with purpose, clarity, and courage—both in uniform and in civilian life. His work spans across education, defence coaching, engineering leadership, and personal growth, where he empowers aspirants and professionals alike to live with integrity and lead with impact.

A proud product of India's rigorous defence training ecosystem, he walked the SSB path not just once—but multiple times, facing rejection, learning from failure, and ultimately earning his recommendation through resilience and reflection.

He went on to serve the nation with dignity and continues to serve in a new uniform—that of a mentor, educator, and guide to thousands of young minds aspiring to become future officers, engineers, and ethical leaders.

His Mission:

To empower 1,00,000 engineers and aspirants to achieve not just exceptional career growth, but also joyful living, financial freedom, and a meaningful contribution to the nation.

He believes that true success lies in automated growth driven by authenticity, and that everyone has the potential to become a leader in their own right.

His Other Books:

- **AUTOMATE YOUR GROWTH**: A 12-Minute Daily Habit to Build Authenticity, Remove Resistance, and Unlock Unstoppable Success

- ***Engineers' Growth Redefined***: *Expertize Uniquely, Communicate Powerfully, and Monetize Effectively in the AI Era*

- **MOVE LIKE WATER**: Bruce Lee's Timeless Lessons to Find Your Flow, Build Your Power, Express Your Authentic Self, Live with Impact

Follow His Journey & Join the Movement:

- Website: www.pradeepkumarkp.com

- YouTube: https://www.youtube.com/@pradeepkumar_k_p

- LinkedIn: https://www.linkedin.com/in/pradeepkumarkp/

- Instagram: https://www.instagram.com/pradeepkumar_k_p/

- Email: ask@pradeepkumarkp.com

DISCLAIMER & ETHICAL DECLARATION

This book, *You're Officer Material: Lessons and Secrets That Help SSB Aspirants Succeed with Clarity, Confidence, and Character*, is intended as a guidance tool for aspirants preparing for the Service Selection Board (SSB) and other officer entry processes into the Indian Armed Forces.

The contents are based on the personal experiences, open-source insights, and public knowledge, research, references, learnings, reflections, and insights of Capt. Pradeepkumar K.P. (Retd.), drawn from his years of service, leadership, and mentorship.

Important Clarifications:

- This book is not officially connected to the Indian Armed Forces, Ministry of Defence, or any SSB centre.

- It does not disclose any confidential procedures. The content is based on personal experience, publicly known formats, and open sources.

- This book does not guarantee selection in the SSB or any defence entry. Success depends on your own preparation, mindset, and performance.

- Its purpose is to help you build clarity, character, and communication—qualities essential for both a military career and good citizenship.

- The author and publisher are not responsible for any result, loss, or consequence—emotional, financial, or professional—that may come from using this book.

Code of Integrity:

As a former officer of the Indian Army, the author is committed to upholding the dignity of the Armed Forces and the selection process. This work is shared in the spirit of service, mentorship, and national pride, with the sole intention of guiding aspirants toward excellence in life and leadership.

Jai Hind!

MAY I ASK YOU FOR A SMALL FAVOR?

First, I want to thank you for reading this book. You could have chosen any other book, but you took mine, and I appreciate this. I hope you have at least a few actionable insights that will positively impact your daily life.

Can I ask for 30 seconds more of your time?

I'd love it if you could leave a review of the book. That will help me grow my readership by encouraging folks to take a chance on my books.

Keeping it straight - reviews are the lifeblood of any author.

It will take less than a minute of your time but will tremendously help me reach out to more people.

If you liked this book, please consider posting an honest review on your preferred retailer, online site or any social media platform. And I'd love to see your review. Thanks for your support.

www.ingramcontent.com/pod-product-compliance
Lightning Source LLC
Chambersburg PA
CBHW051135130726
47988CB00005B/1847